THE RIDGERUNNER
elusive loner of the wilderness

Richard Ripley

PAPERBACKS GALORE
1044 14th Ave.
Longview WA 98632

Backeddy Books

Copyright © 1986 Richard Ripley
All rights reserved.

Cover photograph: Art Wolfe
Cover and interior book design: Debra L. Moloshok

FOREWORD

This story is about a different man who craved a degree of isolation that would crush most people. His lifestyle put him at odds with the federal government and a powerful corporation. He relished those roles, but he is not just another renegade. He pursued his way of life with a dedication that had to be born of desire, not of a compulsion to disagree.

A little bit of his flame burns in each of us. Who has not wanted to change the terms of the world so that wanderlust could be given its nose and the soul could be given more time to enjoy mountains and streams and wild creatures?

The story is also about a different time, when people who worked in the forest relied on their feet to take them places and on their muscles to do their work.

I first heard the story from my father, who is a character in the tale. The story fascinated me because I was lucky enough to visit the Clearwater and St. Joe national forests when their sheer physical dimensions still overwhelmed mankind. In the 1940s, when the story begins, it was possible for an unconventional man to lose himself in the Clearwater and the St. Joe. Those forests are still vast, but they are much too busy now for a person to be so alone.

The story is true. Material for it came mostly from interviews. A Forest Service publication, The Clearwater Story, was an invaluable reference. The description of Paddy McIntyre, who exemplified the hard scrabble side of life in the mountains, comes from Up the Swiftwater by Sandra A. Crowell and David O. Asleson. The account of William Buzzard's flight also comes from that well-researched book. Like McIntyre's description, it is recounted here with permission.

To all who granted their time and their assistance, thank you. I have strived to recreate conversations and occurrences as I was told they happened. My greatest regret is that I could not talk with the Ridgerunner himself. He could not be found.

ONE

Ranger Corland L. James listened at the door of the Roundtop Ranger Station. Hearing nothing, he inserted his key in the lock and turned it. The door swung open. James listened again, but still heard nothing. He went in, followed closely by his companion.

"I don't think there's anyone here, Bill," James whispered.

James' companion, Bill Brown, a part-time Forest Service worker, nodded in agreement.

James slipped his arms from the straps of his packsack and set the bag on the office desk.

"Where did you leave your radio, Bill?" he asked.

"Right here on the desk," Brown said.

"And it was gone when you got back?"

"Yes."

It was May 3, 1942. James was making his first trip of the year to his back-country ranger station. He had come much earlier than he expected, but a thief had broken into the station; James knew that his boss, the supervisor of the St. Joe National Forest, would want a prompt and complete report.

The ranger station sat in the middle of a vast, nearly uninhabited wilderness in north-central Idaho. The nearest town, a railroad village named Avery, was 15 miles to the north. Avery claimed a mere 262 residents. The biggest town in the county, St. Maries, population 2,234, was 50 miles to the west and halfway across the Idaho Panhandle from Avery.

Montana was about the same distance from Roundtop, but to the east. The nearest towns in that direction were on the far side of the steep Bitterroot Divide, across a sea of heavily forested green mountains.

A handful of woodsmen, miners and trappers knew their way across those mountains; they were welcome to use the few cabins that could be found, but they didn't steal things from the spare little buildings.

Brown had discovered the break-in at Roundtop a day earlier, when he arrived to shovel snow from the roofs of the buildings. He had left Avery early in the morning, but returned after making the 30-mile round trip on foot.

The burglary had shaken him, and he had hurried on the return trip, exhausting himself. He staggered as he crossed the concrete bridge over the St. Joe River at Avery's edge.

James, who worked at the Avery Ranger Station while Roundtop was closed for the winter, saw Brown as he came across the bridge. He hadn't expected Brown to return for two days, and he hurried to meet the fatigued man.

"What's wrong?" James asked.

"Been robbed," Brown panted. "Someone broke into the station."

"What!" James exclaimed.

"They took my radio," Brown continued.

"Did you see who it was?"

"No. They were gone when I arrived."

James immediately decided to go to Roundtop the next day. He asked Brown to go with him and also decided to take Paddy McIntyre, an Irishman who had worked for the Forest Service for years.

The three men left for Roundtop before dawn, driving south from Avery on the Kelley Creek Road, which climbed rapidly as it left the canyon of the St. Joe River.

Roundtop's elevation was just short of a mile high; it was snowbound and would be until June. The three men drove until the snow was too deep to take their pickup farther, then strapped on their snowshoes and set off for the ranger station, which was still nine miles away. They were used to walking long distances; they made good time.

About four miles from Roundtop, the road turned downhill; they picked up their pace and maintained it when the road climbed again. Thick stands of spruce, larch, and Douglas fir gave way to dark-green subalpine fir.

James, Brown, and McIntyre paused at the edge of a clearing. The ranger station sat a hundred yards away at the far end of the open area. The round-topped mountain from which the ranger station got its name towered above the handful of buildings.

"Paddy, I want you to check the woods around the clearing for tracks," James said. "Maybe you can pick up the thief's trail. Let us know if you find his tracks. Bill and I will look around the buildings and grounds."

"I'll keep within earshot," McIntyre said. "Give me a yell if you find something." He walked off toward the brush.

When James set his packsack down in the ranger station office a few minutes later, he wondered whether McIntyre had had any luck. The slender little Irishman was an unconventional, uneducated sort who had been around Avery for years, running trap lines in the winter and working as a Forest Service lookout in the summer.

His disdain for soap and water was legendary, as were his woodsmanship and his quirks. A quarter of frozen venison hung over the stove inside his cabin at Bathtub Mountain during the winter; the rising heat from the stove thawed the meat just enough so that he could carve off a steak and drop it into the frying pan when dinner time came.

McIntyre was known for his tracking ability, and as James set to work inside the office, he felt sure the Irishman would find the thief's trail if a trail were there to be found.

"Bill," James said to Brown, "build a fire in the stove and heat some snow in one of the kettles. I'm going to need some water."

James opened the flap on the top of his pack and took out a sack of plaster of Paris mix. Using a pair of scissors he found in his desk, he carefully cut open the bag. Earlier, as he and Brown walked to the ranger station office, James had noticed tracks beside the building; he wanted plaster casts of them.

As he poured the powder into a bowl, James wondered how the thief had approached the station. Maybe he had come along the trail beside the little spring just north of the grounds, hiding momentarily behind the huge barrel the Forest Service used as a cistern. Or perhaps he had sneaked past the barn, where tack and feed were stored for horses and mules. No matter how he came, he would have had good cover behind the head-high brush that surrounded the clearing.

"Here's your water," said Brown.

James took the kettle from Brown and poured some of the lukewarm liquid into the bowl with the plaster of Paris mix. He stirred and added water until the mixture stuck to the sides of the bowl; he carried the bowl outside, picking his way between the patches of dirty late-winter snow in the yard. He went around to the side of the building and stopped beside a window where melting snow dripping from the eaves had softened the ground; the intruder had left distinct footprints in the wet earth.

"Do you suppose he stood here and watched me while I was inside?" Brown asked.

"I don't know, Bill, but he could have," James replied.

"I wouldn't have known," Brown said. His voice betrayed the unease he felt at the thought.

James knelt and began his task while Brown stooped to watch. Daubing two of the footprints with the wet plaster, James noticed that the footprints were small; they looked like those of a woman or a boy.

"Let's take a look around while we wait for these casts to dry," James said, wiping his hands on a towel. "You check the clearing to see if you can find his trail. I'll see if he broke into any of the other buildings."

While Brown inspected the clearing, James examined the ground around the warehouse, cookhouse, and bunkhouse. The thief had taken Brown's radio from the ranger's office, but there were tracks around the other buildings as well. Clusters of them dotted the ground beside each window; apparently, the thief had peered inside all of the buildings before entering the office.

The tracks—made by a pair of boots that James guessed to be a man's size 5 or 6—led in all directions. It looked to James as if the thief wanted to make it difficult for anyone to follow.

"He must be a smart devil," James muttered as he unlocked the padlock on the cookhouse door. As far as James knew, the thief had entered only the ranger's office, but the chances were good that anyone roaming the mountains at this time of year would also look for food.

It was dark inside the two-room log cookhouse, where the Roundtop crew ate during the work season. James let up a shade, and daylight dispelled the darkness. He checked the windows; they were latched and undisturbed.

James walked to the kitchen in the rear of the long building and opened cupboards in which stores were piled. Several boxes of canned goods had been opened, but he was uncertain whether any cans were missing. No inventory was made of the supplies at the end of the season; the cooks might have opened the boxes to prepare meals the previous fall.

"Mr. James, here comes Paddy."

It was Brown, calling from outside. James shut the door and locked it as he left the cookhouse.

McIntyre walked across the yard toward James and Brown, sweat beads covering his glistening face. He had unbuttoned the top buttons of his shirt; it was warmer than the three men had expected.

"I didn't find a thing," McIntyre said as he came up. "He didn't leave a trail. I made a big loop, up on Roundtop Mountain and on the flat all around the station, but I didn't find a single footprint. I don't understand it."

"Catch your breath, Paddy," James replied. "We'll start back as soon as Bill and I pick up our plaster casts and check out the other buildings."

James and Brown turned up no other clues, and the three men started for Avery. It was dark by the time they drove down the hill into town. They stored their gear in the Forest Service warehouse and walked home.

James glanced at the clock on the mantle as he came in out of the cool air. It was 8:17.

"Did you find anything?" Judy James asked her husband.

"Tracks," James said, "tracks everywhere around the buildings, tracks in all directions, but no trail that anyone could follow. Someone broke into the office, all right, but I couldn't tell whether they got into any of the other buildings. I guess we'll have to start making a list of things each fall before we close the station."

It was cool when James walked to work the next morning. He built a fire in the stove in his office, though he knew he wouldn't need the warmth for long. He set a sheet of paper on his desk and looked out the window while he collected his thoughts. He studied the hillside across the St. Joe River and wondered whether the thief was walking across a similar incline elsewhere in the forest. If he was, he would have hard going.

James picked up his pen.

"May 4, 1942," he wrote.

"Traveled from Avery Ranger Station on May 3 with fire guard Paddy McIntyre and Avery resident Bill Brown to Roundtop Ranger Station to investigate illegal entry reported May 2 by Brown. Left pickup 6 miles from Avery and snowshoed 9 miles farther to Roundtop. Arrived at 11:45 a.m.

"No one was at Roundtop, but found footprints in the yard. A radio, personal property of Brown, was missing. Wood from the wood box had been burned and the wood box, left full by Brown the weekend before, was empty. Unsure whether other buildings were entered.

"McIntyre, Brown, and myself searched for the intruder's trail, but had no luck. Made plaster casts of two footprints and will retain in storage for examination by A.J. Cramer, Forest Service regional law enforcement officer.

"Left Roundtop with Brown and McIntyre at 1:55 p.m. Stored gear. Went home at 8 p.m.

"C.L. James,

"District Ranger"

James re-read his memo. The page was half empty, but what else could he say? He addressed an envelope to the forest supervisor, folded the memo, and put it in the envelope.

On a hot July night two months later, James sat at his desk and stared again at a copy of the memorandum. That afternoon he had found further evidence that a stranger was in the forest.

James was walking the nine-mile trail from Roundtop east to the Twin Creeks Cabin to visit two Forest Service workers who were bunking there. No other crew members on his district were stationed farther from Roundtop; James made it a point to check on the two workers often, even though it took several hours to make the trip.

As he walked along, he could see the two rocky ends of Lookout Mountain, which dominated the view of the forest southwest of Roundtop.

Minutes later, Rocky Run Mountain came into view to the southeast. A treeless knob on the mountain reached 4,980 feet. Farther to the south, James knew, were mountains like 5,700-foot Indian Dip and 4,800-foot Buzzard Roost—both part of the St. Joe-Clearwater Divide.

The divide formed a battle line between two geologic fronts, separating two major river drainages—the Clearwater and the St. Joe—and demarking where different natural forces molded the land. On the other side of the divide, the world's largest intrusion of granitic rock stretched from the North Fork of the Clearwater River 300 miles south to Boise. Called the Idaho Batholith, it was formed when a mass of granite exploded upward from the Earth's interior more than 100 million years ago. For centuries, erosion chewed away at the soil atop the intrusion, carving the rugged Clearwater Mountains.

The North Fork of the Clearwater River, which drains the northern end of the batholith, captures the eye with the stark beauty of naked rock and roaring water. The St. Joe Valley, on the other side of the divide, was born in flood rather than explosion. A giant lake once covered the valley, and volcanic lava later flowed through the drainage from eastern Washington.

The mirror-smooth surface of the St. Joe River's lower end reflects the stately trees along its banks; steamboats once cruised its scenic course. In its upper reaches near Avery, the St. Joe turns swift.

While James walked along the trail to Twin Creeks, he looked frequently in the direction of the Clearwater country, and he thought about the remoteness of the 36 miles of timbered mountains between Roundtop and Canyon Ranger Station, the nearest Forest Service office to the south.

In 1884, those mountains provided an escape route for a man who engaged in gunplay with Wyatt Earp and his brothers. The Earps and their adversary, William Buzzard, had opened a saloon in the tent town of Eagle City. Buzzard and the Earps got into a gunfight over a piece of property. Buzzard later surfaced in the town of Pierce on the other side of the divide, and it's probable that Buzzard Roost and a nearby spot called Getaway Point got their names from his flight.

As James hiked, he also thought about how dry the woods were. Anvil-shaped clouds told him that a thunderstorm was coming; the storm might bring dry lightning and start fires.

James was so preoccupied with the weather that he almost walked over a pile of ashes in the trail before he realized what it was. Suddenly, he didn't feel alone. He had instructed his employees not to light fires, even to warm canned food for lunch. The fire must have been set by a stranger.

James knelt to examine the ashes. His gaze fell on an empty tin can. He picked up the can and read the printing on its blackened side. "Lima Beans & Ham, U.S. Govt. Packed and Inspected," the can said. It was from a ration the Forest Service issued to fire-fighters. Such rations were kept in the cookhouse at Roundtop; the can might have been stolen when Bill Brown's radio disappeared in May.

A small flashlight lay in the grass beside the trail. James picked it up; it was a government light—just like the ones in the warehouse at Roundtop. James tried it. It was dead.

"Whoever took Brown's radio must have been in both the cookhouse and the warehouse," James muttered.

The ranger stood. He would hurry on to Twin Creeks, warn the two crewmen there of what he had found, and write a second report that night on the burglary.

Words didn't come easily, however, as James sat at his desk that evening. He was tired, having walked close to 20 miles, and he was worried; every few minutes, lightning interrupted the darkness outside and flared through the window. A fire already might have kindled somewhere in the district.

The phone rang, and James snatched the earpiece off the hook.

"Roundtop," he answered.

"Mr. James?"

"Yes."

"This is the lookout on Fishhook Peak. I think a bolt of lightning hit a snag on Flatiron Knobs due south of Roundtop."

"I'll send out smokechasers," James said.

There was no time to lose. James tossed his unfinished report in a drawer and grabbed his hat off the rack as he went out the door, bound for the bunkhouse. If lightning had hit a dead tree, as often happened, smokechasers would have to get to the spot quickly, or fire might race through the forest.

James never did finish his report. Summer was a busy time for a forest ranger, and the paperwork chore slipped his mind. That fall he accepted a transfer to Florida; the campfire remains he found on the trail went unrecorded in Forest Service files.

Two

Early in the morning of May 4, 1942, two days after Bill Brown discovered the break-in at Roundtop Ranger Station, 18-year-old Bud Ripley packed a duffel bag at his home in Orofino, Idaho. The five-foot, nine-inch youth stuffed the bag with clothing, sundries, and other items he would need during a summer of working in the woods. Trim and well-conditioned, he had manned a lookout tower two summers before and looked forward to working in the forest again. That afternoon he was to start a new job at the Forest Service's Alder Creek Blister Rust Camp, which occupied a broad meadow four miles west of the Potlatch Forests Inc. company town of Headquarters.

Headquarters was 44 miles north and east of Orofino. The road to Alder Creek from Headquarters was too muddy to drive before early June, but Potlatch's rail line—an extensive network used to haul logs from the woods—ran past the camp, and Ripley planned to hitch a ride on a company speeder, a small, box-like rail car that carried personnel through the woods.

Alder Creek was to be the first of two Forest Service work bases for Ripley that summer. The second would be Canyon Ranger Station, a back-country outpost where he would clear trails, string telephone line and fight fires. First, though, he would hand-pull and spray gooseberrry plants, which spread blister rust, a disease that kills white pine.

The camp where Ripley was headed was one of 20 in the Clearwater National Forest where 25-man crews worked to eradicate blister rust. The extensive effort was justified by the high value of white pine, which produces beautiful and workable wood.

Ripley put his bag in the trunk of his late father's metallic gray 1937 Chevrolet sedan and set a new pair of calk boots beside the bag. The boots' soles bristled with bright, shiny nails that provided excellent footing for woods work.

Ripley jumped behind the wheel of the Chevrolet and turned the engine over. It caught, and he waited while it warmed. He slid the choke in, released the brake, pulled onto B Street in front of his home and headed down the hill. He knew he wouldn't be back until the work season ended; he had arranged for a friend to bring the car home.

At the bottom of the hill, Ripley turned onto Michigan Avenue, one of Orofino's busiest streets, and drove the short distance through town to a bridge that spanned the Clearwater River. Ripley turned east and headed up the Clearwater, driving along the river's south bank.

He glanced across the river as he pulled away from the bridge; the name of a local lumber firm, the White Pine Lumber Co., was spelled out in big black letters on the white front of the firm's office. Ripley knew that the firm's name could serve as a calling card for the town of 1,600 people, right down to the species of tree. Orofino's economic lifeblood flowed from the Clearwater country's timber stands.

The highway ran along the south wall of the river's scenic canyon. Six miles east of Orofino, Ripley crossed the river and followed an unpaved road from the hamlet of Greer up the Greer Grade.

The twisting grade wound up the north slope of the river canyon, cutting back so sharply that Ripley could see log trucks approaching far uphill before meeting the trucks in the road's hairpin curves. The road was narrow; driving past the oncoming trucks was nerve-wracking to those who weren't used to the local traffic. Ripley knew the truckers were good drivers, and he paid no heed to the thousand-foot drops off the downhill side of the road.

After Ripley reached the top of the Greer Grade, he drove due east past fields of new wheat on the Weippe Prairie. Mountains ringed the prairie in the distance. Ripley saw that snow still covered Shanghai, a prominent peak that served as an indicator of the seasons as the snow crept up and down its slopes. Soon Shanghai would be bare.

Fifteen miles from Greer, Ripley passed through the little town of Weippe. He turned at the town's main intersection and drove by homes on the northeast side. Most of the homes had gray, aging wood siding. Outside of Weippe, rolling pastures swept away from the road and butted against stands of timber. Ripley watched carefully for stray livestock, which posed a danger to both life and pocketbook since they had the right-of-way.

Eleven miles from Weippe, Ripley came to Pierce, home to lumberjacks and sawmill workers since an early-day gold strike played out. In 1942, 910 people lived in Pierce, which boasted a larger population within months after a party of men led by Capt. E.D. Pierce struck gold in Orofino Creek in 1860.

Ripley drove through Pierce and turned to the northwest. He passed through more rolling country before reaching Headquarters.

Headquarters was the site of Potlatch Forests Inc.'s main logging office in the Clearwater country. The office sat at the south edge of town; across the road, decks of logs stretched for hundreds of yards, waiting to be shipped to Potlatch's mill at Lewiston, Idaho.

Bunkhouses, machine shops, a roundhouse, a mess hall, and three stores stood in Headquarters. So did several houses, in which company employees and their families lived. PFI, as Potlatch Forests Inc. was known, owned every building in town.

Ripley stopped at Headquarters, the automobile part of his trip over. He caught a speeder to the blister-rust camp and settled in for the ride.

His stint at the Alder Creek camp began routinely. He and the other workers who arrived before the main body of the crew felled and limbed small trees to make tent poles for the camp.

A few days later, the cook quit, and Ranger Leroy Lewis assigned Ripley to be the interim cook. Ripley knew next to nothing about cooking. He tried his hand at baking pies and for the first time in his life cut up a quarter of beef, wondering whether he was doing anything right as he hacked away. Luckily, he didn't have to bake bread, as many of the logging-camp cooks did daily.

No one complained about Ripley's meals, but he suspected that his fellow crewmen were being polite. When the weekends came, he was eager to shed his apron and join the other men for a trip to Pierce, where he had no trouble buying drinks in bars crowded with loggers even though he was three years shy of the legal drinking age of 21.

Ripley was relieved when June came and he could leave his kitchen permanently for Canyon Ranger Station. The roads were still soft, but the

Forest Service pickup that came to get him managed to spin its way from the ranger station to a Potlatch camp where he had been taken by a speeder.

On the way to the ranger station, the forest's early season lushness ran by outside the window of the truck. Ripley saw a whitetail deer bound away from the road, flicking its long tail with each leap to warn that an intruder was near.

The road was a torturous, twisting path that jarred passengers mercilessly; a ribbon of bright green grass grew down the middle, and puddles of brown water stood in tracks on either side of the grass. It was impossible to go more than 30 miles per hour, and drivers instinctively looked for turn-outs when oncoming traffic approached. Much of the year mud and snow made the road impassable, and even in the summer a traveler might have to chop a fallen tree out of the way.

The road was the only route to Canyon Ranger Station. It was almost like an entryway into another world, and in a sense that's what it was.

The road crossed the North Fork of the Clearwater 27 miles from Headquarters, joining a two-mile road to Canyon that was the only road in the northern half of the 35-mile long Canyon Ranger District. Vehicles could reach the river at only two other places between the west boundary of the district and the village of Dent, which was 37 miles downstream from the ranger station. Upstream from Canyon the next road to reach the river was at Bungalow Ranger Station, 26 miles away.

Potlatch, the state of Idaho, and the Forest Service owned the forests that lay between Headquarters and the river. Loggers cut trees on the tracts and lived in camps near their work sites, but in the 1940s they had not advanced north of the river in the Canyon district. The mountains there were among the most remote and unused in the United States. While a fisherman or a camper might visit occasionally, most weeks the only vehicle over the road was the supply truck.

It was 36 miles by trail from Canyon to Roundtop on the other side of the St. Joe-Clearwater Divide. Walking was the only way to get between the two points, which was true of most places on the divide. One measure of a Forest Service employee's worth lay in his walking ability.

The divide was utterly wild and home to one of the world's largest elk herds; the stately animals thrived on tender brush that grew after forest fires burned.

In 1910, a huge fire roared 200 miles north from the Salmon River to Wallace, Idaho, in 48 hours, killing 85 people, injuring 115, destroying the east end of Wallace, and devouring back-country railroad and mining towns in its path. The fire hit the St. Joe country especially hard, blackening 2.5 million acres and destroying 5.5 billion board feet of timber.

Fire struck the canyon of the North Fork of the Clearwater in 1919, chasing Jim Gerard, a Forest Service employee, into the river, where he ducked his head repeatedly to escape the heat and flames.

The blaze sucked so much oxygen out of the air that it made Ranger James Urquhart black out. After the fire passed, he came to in the waters of little Elizabeth Creek, where he had fallen.

In the 1940s, gray, branchless tree trunks still stood in long, irregular rows, but because the country was so big and rejuvenated itself so well, the streams ran clear again within a few years after the fires. Their waters were home to spawning steelhead, Chinook salmon and rainbow and cutthroat trout. Ripley looked forward to catching some of the fish, and as the truck crossed the bridge over the North Fork of the Clearwater, he peered down into the river, looking for bull trout that lay in holes near the bridge abutments. He knew the 20-inch fish were there, lazily fanning their tails to hold their position in the current.

For Ripley, the summer's real work was about to begin. The Canyon crew's primary responsibility was fire control; that meant trails had to be cleared so pack trains could carry supplies to the district's 12 lookout towers and crews could reach fires quickly.

It was the same story every spring: Aging trees that were too big for the horses and mules to get over had fallen during the winter, blocking the trail, and snow-laden limbs had torn down many of the phone lines that linked the ranger station to the lookout towers. Run-off from deep snow in the high country had washed out bridges and unleashed slides. Rocks had rolled onto the trails, the brush was encroaching from the sides, and the paths needed to be smoothed. There were many trails, and they had to be kept in excellent shape; they provided the only lines of communication to most parts of the district.

As the days grew hotter, most of the crewmen would move to the mountain-top lookouts. Ripley and two crewmen named George Martindale and Willmont "Arky" Turner would continue to work on trails and string phone line when they weren't fighting fires.

The district owned just two vehicles, a pickup and an old truck that ran temperamentally. The crewmen walked wherever they went and had no power tools to make their work easier. Their most difficult job was sawing, which was done with the crosscut saw, nicknamed the "misery whip." The long, two-man saw left new crewmen panting after a few minutes of work. The secret was to avoid binding the springy blade while one's partner pulled it through a log from the other side.

Carrying such tools was almost as demanding as using them. In addition to the crosscut saw, packed over the shoulder with its garish rakers pointed away from the neck, the crewmen carried axes, wedges, steel tree-climbing spurs, wire cutters, and log-rolling tools called peaveys. A steel point and a heavy steel hook made up the business end of the peavey; when clamped around a log, the hook held securely, but it made the peavey heavy.

On June 9, Ranger Leroy Lewis told Ripley and Martindale to set up a camp on the circuitous, 12-mile trail from the North Fork to Goat Ridge Lookout. Once their camp was established, the two were to clear trails in the vicinity and re-string phone line.

As Ripley and Martindale hiked down the road from Canyon, they could count the rounded, white and green rocks on the bottom of the river even though the rocks were under 10 feet of water. They marveled at the river's clarity and threw small rocks across. It took a good throw to reach the other side.

They left the road where it turned onto the bridge across the river and followed a trail until it crossed the mouth of Isabella Creek. Tall cedars grew in a glade on the west side of Isabella Creek, and huge, sunlight-dappled ferns hid the ground.

The trail steepened. They hiked up through the trees, crossed an open hillside, then went down into another timbered draw. The trail rose and fell. They came to a spring that seeped out of the hillside, turning the ground into a muddy ooze. A log footbridge had failed years ago; Ripley and Martindale would have to repair it.

The bridge had been in place since not long after the Forest Service built the main trail along the North Fork in 1924. In the 1870s, the Northern Pacific Railroad built the first trail along the North Fork when it surveyed the river for a rail-line route. The company reported that the rough terrain made the survey one of the most difficult ever undertaken in the United States.

Ripley and Martindale walked on from the spring. A short distance away, they came to the confluence of Isabella Creek and little Fern Creek.

A white canvas tent, folded in a tight bundle, sat in the huckleberry brush off the trail next to wooden boxes of food and kitchenware. Two shovels, a pair of climber's spurs, an ax, and a crosscut saw leaned against the boxes. The packer had brought the equipment that morning.

An abandoned prospector's shack sat nearby; Martindale wrestled his pack off his back and set it against the wall of the little gray building.

"We'll put our food in the shack and sleep in the tent," he said. "Okay?"

"That sounds fine to me," Ripley said.

Ripley backed up to a tree stump, set his pack on the stump, pulled his arms from the straps, turned, and caught the pack as it tipped forward. He rubbed his shoulders where the pack's straps had ridden. While Martindale put the food away, Ripley cut tent poles. Then they pitched the tent. They were tightening the last of the strings on the tent's walls when Arky Turner, another of the Canyon crewmen, came up the trail.

"Hello," Martindale said. "I thought this was an isolated part of the woods."

"A notice came in the mail from the Selective Service System this morning," Turner replied. "You've got to take a physical for the draft, George. The ranger opened the envelope as soon as he saw who it was from. He said for you to go back to the station and he will drive you out of the woods tomorrow."

"Does he know how long I'll be gone?" Martindale asked.

"At least three days," Turner said. "They give the physicals at Spokane. I'm supposed to work here with Bud until you get back."

After Martindale left, Ripley and Turner worked their way back down the trail to the river, cutting brush, tossing rocks out of the way, and smoothing the path. It was late afternoon when they reached the river; they turned back for camp.

They slept well that night. Ripley woke when raindrops popped against the taut canvas roof, but he drifted off again. In the morning, it drizzled while Turner mixed canned milk and eggs and cooked the meal over a fire. They drank hot, black coffee and ate thick slices of toasted homemade bread, which the packer had brought from the ranger station. By 6 a.m. it was light and they were on their way to the spring where the bridge had failed.

At the spring, they felled and limbed eight-inch trees, which were sturdy enough to serve as a frame for a new bridge. They wrestled the trees out of the woods, lifting them over rocks and stumps, and dropped them so their ends rested on either side of the mudhole. They dug short, shallow trenches to secure the ends of the trees and lined the trenches with flat rocks so they wouldn't erode. When the trees were in place, they cut smaller logs, sawed them into pieces and used their axes to lop off the logs' rounded edges. They set the logs atop the two trees on their flat sides. The small logs rested solidly, forming a floor for the bridge.

They planned to cut two more trees and lay them atop the small logs to hold them in place, but it was noon and they were hungry.

A light rain had fallen all morning, and they were wet from the rain and their own sweat.

"Let's go back to camp and build a fire so we can dry out while we eat," Turner said.

They hiked the eighth of a mile to their camp. Since Turner had prepared breakfast, it was Ripley's turn to cook. Ripley planned to heat a can of soup, but as he opened the door of the prospector's shack, he froze.

Cans were strewn about and the flour sack had been upended. An egg carton, empty, lay upside down on the floor.

"Arky, come quick!" Ripley called.

"What's the matter?" Turner said.

"Look!"

"No animal did this," Turner said. "An animal would have made a worse mess and eaten part of its plunder."

Turner brushed past Ripley, went inside, and threw open the doors of the cupboards. His hands banged cans and boxes together as he inventoried the loss.

"Let's check the tent," he said, his eyes hard as flint. Ripley followed.

Turner's sleeping bag lay on the ground inside the tent, and his duffel bag gaped open. Three boot socks Ripley had left lying on the ground in the corner were missing. So were a Forest Service packsack and sleeping bag.

Ripley lifted the head of his sleeping bag from his cot. His new .22-caliber High Standard pistol was still there. So was his Kodak camera.

"Who could it have been?" he asked. "Nobody came up the trail this morning, and there's no other way in here."

"I don't know," Turner answered. "Let's see if we can catch him."

Turner tore the tent fly out of his way as he stormed outside. He strode up the trail, but stopped abruptly.

"Look, Bud," he said, pointing at the trail. Footprints marked the damp earth in the middle of the trail; they had been made by someone wearing a small pair of boots.

Turner broke a short, heavy branch from a dead tree that lay next to the trail. The branch was hard and thick; it would make a good club. Turner walked on.

The forest was quiet; the two men could hear the brush swish against their pantlegs as they hurried along. Water from the wet leaves soaked their pantlegs, which clung to their calves.

Turner stopped abruptly; Ripley almost ran into him from behind.

"We can't follow him here," Turner said. "It's too rocky."

He tossed his club into the brush.

"Come on, Bud," he said. "Let's go tell the ranger what happened."

Turner walked back toward the camp, but Ripley stood looking up the trail for a moment. The mist had lifted and it had stopped raining. Ripley listened. All he could hear was Isabella Creek's persistent rushing.

Ripley wondered who could be in the drainage. Isabella Creek ran through a narrow, dark canyon that was as rough a place as he had ever seen. Upstream, thousands of fallen trees toppled years before by violent wind covered the steep slopes of the canyon, defying travelers who were in a hurry. It was 11 miles from where Ripley stood to the Goat Ridge Lookout, and it was many miles farther to the cabins, lookouts, and ranger stations on the other side of the St. Joe-Clearwater Divide. Since the thief had not come up from the river, he must have come down from the divide.

He might be dangerous, Ripley knew. "I guess I should have brought my pistol from the tent," he thought.

He turned and followed Turner back toward the camp, taking a last look over his shoulder.

T*HREE*

The thief struck again on July 11, a month and a day after he hit the tent camp at Isabella Creek. This time his victim was Bill Faucheaux, the lookout at Goat Ridge. Faucheaux's lookout was the only sign of civilization on the treeless, 6,372-foot ridge. An act of thievery could unnerve someone living alone in so remote a place; as soon as Ripley heard about the theft, he telephoned Faucheaux, with whom he had become friends.

As he sat down to use the telephone at the ranger station, Ripley could see Faucheaux's squat, two-story lookout building in his mind. Even though the building was not atop a tower like most lookouts, it afforded a view for miles. It sat on the ridge's sharp, rocky backbone, well above the timber line.

Ripley plugged a phone line into a connection on the switchboard and rang two longs, the number at Goat Ridge. "Goat Ridge," Faucheaux answered.

"Bill, this is Bud. I hear you've joined the ranks of us crime victims."

"Hello, Bud," Faucheaux replied. "I just made a pot of coffee. Why don't you come up and have a cup with me?"

Ripley laughed. Faucheaux knew that Ripley had just returned to Canyon after spending a week on the trail; Ripley would be uninterested in walking 14 miles.

"Where were you when the thief came?" Ripley asked.

"I was on a fire. The lookout on Indian Dip over in the St. Joe reported two little smokes down the hill from me. I left to put them out. When I got back, he had been here and left."

"Do you think he set the fires to get you out of your lookout?"

"Maybe."

"Did he take your new pistol?"

"Yes. I sure hated to lose that gun."

Faucheaux had bought a new .32-caliber automatic pistol before coming to the woods; he was proud of the weapon.

"What else did he take?"

"He took a box of shells and my blue Mackinaw, my raincoat, two pairs of undershorts, four cans of Velvet tobacco, some canned fruit, and a brick of cheddar cheese. The packer had just brought that cheese; I was really looking forward to it."

"I'll bet."

"You know what?" Faucheaux added. "He also took a bath while he was here and shaved with my razor. The basin was full of whiskers, and there was soapy water all over the counter."

"Really?"

"Really."

That part of Faucheaux's story surprised Ripley; obviously, the thief was very bold.

"The ranger took statements from Turner and me after our tent camp was hit," Ripley said. "Did he take a statement from you?"

"Yes. He came the day after the robbery. We talked here."

Ripley pictured the one-room fire-watch area and living quarters in Faucheaux's lookout. Windows made up the upper half of the walls on all four sides of the room, allowing unimpeded visibility. A small wood stove sat against one wall. A bunk sat in one corner, a desk in another.

A chest-high metal fire finder with a circular map tray dominated the center of the room. When a fire broke out, the lookout lined up the sights of the fire finder with the smoke emitted by the fire, then telephoned the fire's coordinates to the ranger station, where the station crew plotted them with coordinates reported by other lookouts. The system was a good way to pinpoint a fire, no easy task for lookouts who watched over a confusing maze of timber-covered ridges.

Faucheaux interrupted Ripley's thoughts.

"After your tent was robbed, did you worry about whether the thief was watching you from the brush?" he asked. "The guy could be around, and you'd never know it."

"I've wondered about that a time or two," Ripley replied. "Early this year I was trying to pull a phone line out from under a snowdrift near your lookout. I had brushed the trail and re-strung the phone line all the way from my camp, and I wanted to finish the job, but I couldn't get the last section of line out from under that snowdrift no matter how hard I tried. Finally, I reefed on it as hard as I could and lost my grip and fell over backwards down the hill. When I got up, I had a funny feeling that someone was watching me. I looked around, but didn't see anyone. Maybe I just felt sheepish about falling on my backside."

"You haven't seen any strange tracks or other odd signs since you were robbed?"

"No."

"I heard you had a bear in your camp."

"We did. He cleaned us out a lot worse than the thief did. You should have seen the mess. I also saw a bear on Eagle Point. I was looking down to watch my footing and didn't see him until I almost ran into him. I heard a whoof and looked up; he was only about 10 feet away. I didn't know I could stop that fast."

"What did he do?"

"He looked at me a minute, then took off into the brush."

"I've still got some of that banana oil and creosote you and Walt Shriner brought from town while we were at fire school on Elk Mountain," Faucheaux said. "That stuff sure kept the bugs off of us. I thought the noseeums were going to eat us alive up there. It's amazing how they come right through a window screen and get into your sleeping bag. Until you fellows brought that goop, I don't think anybody got much sleep."

"It was too hot to sleep," Ripley said.

"Have you been on many fires?" Faucheaux asked.

"I've been on two lightning strikes near The Nub. Neither one amounted to much. The ranger was going to send me to another fire up on Five Lakes Butte in the middle of the night. I wasn't looking forward to that trip. He changed his mind and told me I could wait until morning, but I couldn't find the fire. It must have burned itself out."

"How's the fishing?"

"It's been good. I caught my limit where Collins Creek and Skull Creek run together. They were all rainbows and cutthroats. A couple were longer than 20 inches."

"What's the limit on trout? Twenty-five a day?"

"Yes."

"And you caught them all in one hole."

"Uh huh. One of the guys caught his limit there, fell down and lost his fish in Skull Creek on the way home, then went back and caught another limit out of the same hole. It's a good spot."

"It must be," Faucheaux said. "Sometimes I wish I was closer to water, and not just so I could fish. Packing water every day gets tiresome."

"How far do you have to go for it?"

"Three quarters of a mile. I get it from a spring down the hill. Since it's so far, I carry five gallons at a time on my back. Then I don't have to make the trip more than once a day."

"When I was on the Bertha Hill Lookout two summers ago we had to go a quarter of a mile to an old logging camp for water," Ripley said. "Some of the buildings at the camp were still standing. One of them had an old Monarch wood stove in it."

"I suppose you heard that I've been drafted," Faucheaux said.

"Yes, I did. When are you leaving?"

"At the end of the week. I'll catch the train at Spokane. I'm going directly to Fort Leonard Wood, Missouri, for basic training."

"I'm sorry to see you go."

The two men talked briefly about the war before ending their conversation. Ripley was satisfied that the burglary hadn't rattled Faucheaux. The incident troubled Ranger Roy Lewis, however. The normally easygoing Lewis feared that the thief would harm a member of the district crew.

The tall, fortyish ranger, a veteran of several years with the Forest Service, had run the Canyon Ranger Station since 1936. Before that he served several seasons at the Lochsa Ranger Station, which was on a tributary of the Clearwater River. Lewis knew his woodcraft, and after the thefts at Isabella Creek and Goat Ridge, he kept his eyes open for strangers as he glided along the forest trails, which he walked with unusual speed because of his long stride. For weeks, he saw no one who even remotely raised his suspicions. Then, on Aug. 7, he personally discovered a third theft. This time, the thief had hit the Collins Creek Cabin.

The remote cabin, a 10-mile walk from Canyon, was one of many single-room log buildings in which Forest Service crewmen bunked as they went about the forest. The Forest Service kept a wood-burning stove, two single beds, dishes, and inexpensive furniture in the cabins. A small supply of canned food could be found under a trap door in the floor.

As soon as Lewis opened the door of the cabin, his eyes fell on items from a smokechaser's pack sitting out of place on the bedsprings of one of the two bunks. The mattress from the bunk lay on the floor.

"What's going on?" the ranger muttered to himself, but he already knew. The thief had struck again.

It irritated Lewis that the thief had gotten into a smokechaser's pack.

The packs were kept ready for use at a moment's notice; if a smokechaser arrived at a fire without an ax or other important tool, it could mean that a fire would get away.

Hurriedly, Lewis looked through the items on the bedsprings. A map case, compass, and first-aid kit were missing, and so was the packsack that they belonged in. He picked up the mattress and set it back on the bedsprings.

Lewis lifted the trap door in the floor and felt around in the small food cellar. He couldn't tell whether any food was missing; he found only a few tins, but crewmen working in the area might have used much of the food supply.

Lewis examined the padlock and the hasp on the door; neither was even scratched. He turned his attention to the window at the back of the building; it was secure, its white casing unmarked. The intruder must have used the door to get in. There was no sign, however, that the door had been forced open. Apparently, the man opened locks with ease.

Lewis went outside; the ground gave no indication where the thief had walked. Lewis followed Skull Creek, which ran behind the cabin, for about 20 yards to its junction with Collins Creek. He still found no tracks and walked back down the swift, narrow stream, stopping at a horse corral two dozen paces downstream from the cabin. He searched the ground around the corral, but again found nothing. Discouraged, he locked the cabin and left, making a mental note to have someone replace the items taken from the smokechaser's pack.

Four nights later, on Aug. 11, another burglary occurred. Wayne Shriver and Teddy Tucker, who had moved in at Goat Ridge after Faucheaux left, slept soundly on the second floor of the lookout building while someone entered the ground-floor storage room and stole coffee, cheese, two boxes of cereal, a canned ham, and a flashlight. The other crewmen teased Shriver and Tucker, saying that they slept too soundly, but Lewis did not join in the kidding. He was worried about his employees.

The ranger discovered another break-in on Sept. 12. Rain had eased the fire danger in late August, and Lewis had called the lookouts in for the season on Sept. 2. He and packer Clarence Stevenson rode into the mountains several days later to lock up the Goat Ridge and Smith Point lookouts. Everything was in order at Goat Ridge, but as Lewis and Stevenson rode up to the Smith Point tower, they saw footprints in the soil.

Lewis reined in his mount and slipped out of the saddle to examine the footprints. They were medium-sized, about a man's size 8. A boot with a corrugated composition sole and a rounded heel had made them. The thief had changed footwear since he struck at Isabella Creek in June, but Lewis had no doubt it was the same man.

It had rained 48 hours earlier, and the prints were made after it rained. A kapok sleeping bag, coffee, cheese, lard, and a small amount of dried cereal had been taken from a storage shack that sat in the shadow of the 100-foot tower.

Lewis' curiosity about the thefts remained keen during the winter months. He asked his fellow rangers whether they had experienced similar problems, but learned nothing until he talked with Merrill Oaks, the new ranger at Roundtop.

"We had five cases of thievery last summer, and I wouldn't be surprised if the thief has stolen some things since I buttoned up the ranger station for the winter," Lewis told Oaks. "Have you had problems, too?"

"I think I know of the fellow you're talking about, Roy," Oaks replied. "Corland James, my predecessor, made a trip to Roundtop early last year to check on the theft of a crewman's radio. When I took over as ranger, I ran across James' report, and I got to checking with the men. Somebody broke into the Peewee Cabin in the Red Ives Ranger District between March 10 and March 15 the year before the radio was taken. The thief stole several items that belonged to John Dennis, who works for the Forest Service and was spending some time in the woods in the off-season. Since Dennis wasn't on agency time, few Forest Service people knew about the theft, but they know about it now. We've had other incidents, and people have taken to calling the thief the Ridgerunner."

"The Ridgerunner?"

"Yes. It's a name that comes from the South, where it's been tagged onto moonshiners and crazy men who roam the hills; it seems to have stuck."

"So he was in the woods in March of '41?"

"It sure looks that way."

"Where is the Peewee Cabin?"

"It's halfway between Avery and Red Ives, which is 40 miles up the 'Joe' from Avery. Apparently, after he took Dennis's things he went from the Peewee Cabin over Bathtub Mountain and Bear Skull Mountain to Roundtop and broke into the office there."

"How far is that," Lewis asked, "about 40 miles?"

"About that," Oaks said. "He can travel. I found that out last month."

"What happened?"

"I saw him."

"You saw him?"

"That's right. I chased him, too. I almost caught him, but he got away."

"Did you get a good look at him?"

"No."

"Tell me about it."

"I rode in to Roundtop last month. I was itching to get in there since it was my first season as ranger. Howard Higgins from Avery went with me. We were worried that the snow might make for a long trip, but there wasn't much snow, and the footing for the horses was good.

"We got to the ranger station just as it was starting to get dark. Evidently the Ridgerunner wasn't expecting anyone, because he was in the ranger's office."

Oaks' early season visit to Roundtop had surprised the secretive man who had been walking the trails of the St. Joe and Clearwater forests.

The man had entered the ranger's office 15 minutes before Oaks' arrival, moving briskly as he crossed the clearing around the station. He had watched the ranger station since the middle of the previous day; he expected it had been months since anyone was in the buildings, but he wanted to make sure he was alone.

The man entered the office and closed the door. He waited several moments for his eyes to adjust to the darkness before he started to move about. He stepped to the left into the room where the ranger's desk sat. He opened a drawer in the desk and found a pair of wool socks rolled up in a ball. He stuffed the socks into his coat and turned his attention to the shelf against the wall, where records were kept but other items sometimes could be found. He spotted two boxes of fire rations and slipped the rations inside his coat next to the socks. He continued looking through the shelves for a flashlight, batteries, or other useful items. Suddenly, a horse whinnied.

The man tensed. He knew the horse hadn't come into the mountains alone. He had no doubt that its rider was headed for the ranger's office. He didn't want to show himself, but unless he fled, he might be trapped.

The man wheeled and made for the door, knocking over a chair in the process. He pulled the fire rations and socks from his coat and dumped them onto the floor as he went. He tore open the door, leaped off the porch, and raced across the frozen snow toward the brush at the edge of the clearing.

Oaks saw the man as soon as he emerged from the building.

"It's the Ridgerunner," the ranger yelled to his companion, who was trailing him.

Oaks' mare saw the running figure at the same time her rider did. She shot straight up, pawing the air with her front hooves. Oaks' partner also lost control of his mount momentarily.

"Whoa," the two men yelled at their horses as the animals stomped the ground and spun.

Oaks brought his horse under control first. He kicked her sides, and the mare galloped to the spot where the running man had disappeared into the brush.

Oaks jumped down from his mount. "Grab my horse, Howard," Oaks yelled as he ran into the brush.

Like Lewis, Oaks was a tall man. His long legs made him a swift runner, and he was well-conditioned; he thought he had a good chance of catching the intruder, but it would be hard to see the fleeing man in the brush.

Oaks looked intently in the direction the man had gone. He heard a noise. It was the sound of crunching snow, well ahead in the brush. The ranger ran toward the sound, pushing himself to top speed as quickly as he could. He dodged the brush as he raced past. His boots broke through the crust of snow with each stride and mashed the dry, frozen pine needles underneath.

A dark figure raced up and over a small ridge three dozen paces ahead. It was hard for Oaks to make out the running figure in the shadows. Oaks ran harder. He topped the little ridge and saw that the man had crossed a small draw and started up another ridge.

The man was headed for the canyon of the Little North Fork of the Clearwater River, a mile and a half from Roundtop. If he got below the snow line in the canyon, he would be hard to follow. Oaks was certain that he could overtake the man on level, clear ground, but the ranger couldn't run flat out through the brush. The foliage tore at his face and arms, while the running figure ahead seemed to miss every branch and rock. Oaks also sensed that the man felt a tremendous fear.

"Stop," Oaks yelled. "I won't hurt you." The man paid no heed.

The two men ran on through the dark forest, but Oaks could get no closer to his quarry. If Higgins realized where the man was headed, he might cut him off by riding ahead on the trail that ran south from Roundtop. The man wasn't covering ground as fast as he had at first, but Oaks was slowing down, too. He pushed himself, but still he could not gain on the man.

Suddenly, the end of a broken branch caught Oaks' coat by the shoulder, causing him to lurch sideways. He kept his feet and saw the man run out of the timber and cross the trail. Higgins couldn't cut him off now. He was headed downhill into the canyon.

Oaks' throat was dry. He put his last ounce of energy into the run. As he bounded across the trail, his foot hit a rock and he fell, tucking his shoulder just before he hit the ground. He rolled over onto his back. He had fallen hard. He hurt all over, but he scrambled to his feet as the man vanished into the timber down the hill. He would soon be below the snow line.

Oaks renewed the chase, reaching the trees in a few moments and continuing on, trying to catch a glimpse of the running man. Oaks' long legs, however, were no advantage when it came to running downhill. Each stride jolted his frame, and his heart pounded as if it were going to explode. He had to rest. He ran out onto a grassy knoll and stopped, bending at the waist and putting his hands on his knees to take in big gulps of air. He stood, still breathing hard.

Oaks could neither hear nor see the man; nor could he see the man's tracks. To make matters worse, the darkness was growing. He knew the chase was over. If he hadn't fallen, he might have kept the man in sight, but he doubted that he would have caught him. The fellow was like a rabbit going through the brush. Oaks turned to climb back up the hill.

Not far away, a darkly clothed figure slipped out of a hollow tree trunk. The eight-foot tree trunk, left standing years earlier when a bolt of lightning blasted into a hemlock tree, had made a perfect hiding place. The man had stood inside and waited while the long-legged ranger ran past. Now the man was going to set a zig-zag trail through the rugged canyon.

If a search party came, he wouldn't be easy to find. He would double back on his trail to make sure he wasn't being followed. Then, when the search party gave up, he would go south through the rugged, densely forested mountains to the Clearwater country, a trip he had made before.

Oaks dragged himself to the top of the hill, where Higgins waited with the horses.

"Lost him, huh?" Higgins said.

"Yes, but we'll get a crew in here and keep looking," Oaks said.

The two men returned to the ranger station and radioed for help. That afternoon three Forest Service men arrived.

One of the men paired up with Oaks and the other two stayed together. The two search teams combed the canyon of the Little North Fork for three days. They found tracks leading away from the hollow tree where the man had hidden, but could not follow the tracks very far. Obviously, the fellow was clever.

As the searchers walked up a hillside on the final day of their hunt, a pair of black eyes watched from high up in a nearby tree.

"If we don't have any luck today, we'll give up," Oaks said. "We can't stay out here for the rest of the winter."

After the two men went over the crest of the hill, the man in the tree waited for a half hour, listening and watching intently. Then he slipped out of the tree and headed south.

It would be a long, hard trip. A storm could come up at any time, but he knew where he was going, and if he were pursued he had many places to hide. He doubted that anyone would follow him. He had never encountered another person while crossing the St. Joe-Clearwater Divide in the winter.

"We looked for him for three days and found nothing other than a footprint or two," Oaks told Lewis as he concluded his story.

"I don't like having him around," Lewis said. "He might hurt someone."

"That worries me, too," Oaks said.

Four

After their conversation in the winter of 1942-43, Lewis and Oaks agreed to contact one another when the thief struck. They didn't have to wait long.

In early May, the thief stole a pair of field glasses, two compasses, and food from Roundtop Ranger Station. That same month Lewis arrived at Canyon to find a shutter ripped from an office window and a pane broken from the window. The thief had taken food from the building, which also served as a cookhouse and commissary, and dripped candle wax from room to room.

On July 7, Canyon dispatcher Lloyd Leach found tracks in a lingering patch of snow near the lookout on The Nub. An intruder had built a fire in a nearby cabin, but took nothing.

Two days later, crewmen working east of Canyon found that a sleeping bag and canned foods had been taken from the Skull Creek Cabin.

Frank Marquette, an old prospector who lived on a mining claim six miles down the river from Canyon, told Lewis that someone had cut the seat out of a new pair of overalls he had left hanging out to dry. The intruder also built a fire in Marquette's woodshed and stole two hats and a sack of beans after breaking the lock on the prospector's door.

Lewis had had enough. In August, he proposed that the Forest Service make a concerted effort to catch the Ridgerunner.

"Should this man or men continue to pilfer I am certain that it will be difficult to hire young boys who will be willing to stay alone on lookouts another season," Lewis said in a memorandum to Clearwater National Forest Supervisor Percy Melis. "I would recommend that four to six rangers from the St. Joe and the Clearwater comb the back country by foot sometime during the coming winter. Besides this, a plane could be used to try to locate the intruder. Perhaps then a stop can be put to this continued pilfering."

No search was made, however.

Four more instances of thievery occurred in 1943. Sometime between Sept. 5 and Sept. 8, a .22-caliber bolt-action rifle was stolen from the Skull Creek Cabin.

On Sept. 8, some 42 miles across the St. Joe-Clearwater Divide, an intruder stole 15 fire rations, 10 pounds of flour, and 8 cans of corned beef from Roundtop. He also took beans, bread, tea, crackers, and a packsack, apparently to carry his plunder.

Packers Clarence Stevenson and Dick Van Cleve just missed the thief while he was at work in October. They arrived at the Collins Creek Cabin to find that the shutters were dislodged and the cabin's only window was open.

Stevenson and Van Cleve found a pair of field glasses and a flashlight inside the cabin. They suspected that the thief wouldn't have left the items behind—nor left the window open—unless he had been in a hurry.

The two packers picked up the field glassses and flashlight with rags to preserve fingerprints, and Lewis made sure he didn't touch them with his bare hands when he sent them to Missoula for examination. In a message he enclosed, Lewis wrote that the man who left the items evidently was the same intruder who had been "molesting" Forest Service installations in the Clearwater and the St. Joe.

"By all indications," Lewis wrote, "the field glasses and flashlight had been stored or hung in a damp place, possibly in a cave or improvised shelter, as the cases on each were molded."

Forest Service law enforcement officer A.J. Cramer determined that the field glasses were the same ones that had been stolen from Roundtop in May. The glasses carried the Forest Service brand. On Nov. 30, Oaks discovered yet another burglary at Roundtop. This time the thief had taken 20 pounds of flour, 25 fire rations, and a half slab of bacon.

By now the pilfering had become a hot topic on the streets of Headquarters, Pierce, Weippe, and Orofino, and, on the other side of the divide, in Avery, St. Maries, and Calder, which was up the St. Joe midway between St. Maries and Avery.

The idea that a man was living year-round in the rugged divide caught the imagination of the residents of the timber towns, many of whom made their living in the woods. They knew that snow drifted to 20 feet deep in the divide in the winter, and wind gunned ice crystals over the ridgetops. Few woodsmen visited the divide at that time of year, but in the winter of 1942-43, pilots watched for tracks on the mountaintops—and found them.

Speculaton about the Ridgerunner abounded. Artful conversationalists said he was a giant and a killer. A few years earlier, the FBI had checked the St. Joe country for a suspect in the Mattson kidnapping, in which a Tacoma doctor's daughter had been taken in 1937. The suspect had once worked in the St. Joe, and it was believed he might have hidden there to avoid questioning.

State and county law-enforcement officers suspected that a convicted murderer named "Baldy" Weber was hiding in the Clearwater National Forest. Weber had escaped from prison not long before and boasted in a Weippe bar that he would not be taken alive; he warned that he was going to hole up in the woods and shoot anyone who tried to arrest him.

Some people thought the Ridgerunner was a draft dodger. Draft dodgers occasionally sought refuge in mountainous areas during World War II, although few chose sanctuaries as remote as the St. Joe-Clearwater Divide.

The residents of the logging towns saw nothing wrong with the Ridgerunner's use of back-country cabins. The story spread that he used only what he needed and left the cabins clean and stocked with firewood. Lewis and Oaks knew that wasn't the case, but they had greater worries. A number of Forest Service employees took their wives and children into the woods each summer, and women worked in the logging camps. The Ridgerunner might be a rapist or child molester who would strike if he had the chance.

Since the Ridgerunner roamed a wide area and traveled the forest with apparent ease, the Forest Service needed a line on his whereabouts to make a search succeed. Finally, on March 30, 1944, a break came.

Lewis had sent Clyde Cole and Louis Holt into the woods to evaluate the work needed to open Canyon for the summer. The ranger instructed the two men to watch for signs of illegal entry and carry rifles.

It was late in the day as Cole and Holt hiked up the North Fork to the Flat Creek Cabin, where they intended to spend the night. The cabin was midway between Canyon and Bungalow Ranger Station, and the next day they planned to walk the 13 miles to the Bungalow, where they would end their trip.

The two men were hungry and eager to stop for the evening, but as they approached the cabin smoke streamed from the building's steep, gabled roof, breaking the line of darkened tree tops on the horizon. Cole and Holt knew that no one with the Forest Service was in the woods, and as soon as they saw the smoke they were on their guard.

"Let's look in the window," Cole whispered.

The two men crept to the side of the building and peered inside. Someone was sitting at the table in the cabin, eating.

The man sat so he faced the door. He was sideways to Cole and Holt and looking down. He did not see the Forest Service men, and they could not make out his face.

Cole and Holt moved away from the window to avoid being seen. Holt tapped Cole on the shoulder and indicated that they should go around to the door. Cole nodded. The two men quietly slipped to the front of the cabin.

"I don't think he knows we're here," Holt whispered. "Let's go in quickly."

The two men stepped up on the porch gingerly, then threw the door open and strode inside.

They obviously had taken the stranger by surprise; he held his fork in mid-air.

"Hello," Holt said. He closed the door without turning his back to the stranger and set the butt of his rifle on the floor and held the weapon by its barrel. Cole, who had come through the door behind Holt, cradled his rifle in his arms.

The stranger said nothing. Holt and Cole still could not see his face. The cabin was lit by a single, flickering candle that sat on the floor under the table; the table subdued much of the light from the candle.

The two Forest Service men glanced around the cabin quickly. A rifle rested against the table. Canned Forest Service rations sat in a small stack in one corner of the table. The man had intended to add to his food supply.

Beneath the table, where the candle cast most of its light, Holt and Cole could see the man's boots and pantlegs. His boots were cracked and aged, and his wool pants were badly worn. Clearly, the fellow had been leading a difficult existence. Holt and Cole knew that they had found the Ridgerunner.

They wanted to see the man's face badly, but it was in shadow, and he wore his hat pulled low on his brow. The candle burned a little brighter for an instant, and they got a glimpse of his eyes, which flashed so brightly that their intensity struck Holt and Cole.

The Ridgerunner still had not responded to Holt's greeting. Nor had he made any other sound or moved.

"Why are you using this cabin?" Cole asked evenly.

The man put down his fork. His reply came quickly. "I've got to feed my horses," he said. "Then we can eat together."

He pushed back from the table and stood. He grabbed his rifle by the sling and threw the gun over his shoulder. His movements were nimble and quick. He stepped between Holt and Cole, opened the door, and went out into the night, closing the door behind him.

"What should we do?" Holt asked. "He doesn't have any horses and he has no intention of coming back."

"Let's radio Pierce," Cole replied.

Cole wrestled his packsack off his back and dug into it feverishly. He pulled out a portable radio and switched the set on; it crackled with static.

"Pierce Ranger Station, come in please," Cole said. "This is Clyde Cole. Louis Holt and I just surprised the Ridgerunner in the Flat Creek Cabin."

It took hours to ascertain that Holt and Cole had the authority to arrest the Ridgerunner, and by that time it was too late to pursue him. Percy Melis, the Clearwater forest supervisor, decided that a Forest Service employee named Moton Roark would pick up the Ridgerunner's trail the next day. He ordered Holt and Cole to continue their trek out of the woods in the morning.

The quiet, polite-spoken Roark was one of the few local woodsmen who had a reputation rivaling that of the Ridgerunner. In the conversations at the Forest Service stations and in town, it seemed to Roark that all people talked about was the Ridgerunner.

As he listened to the stories, Roark thought, "I can go anywhere anyone else can go. If I can just get on his trail, I can catch him."

In truth, Roark had a growing yen to match himself against the forest stranger. Roark knew the North Fork as well as anyone; he was an expert tracker and kept his 5-foot, 10-inch body in top condition. He avoided alcohol and tobacco, and at 47, after coming west in the '20s to escape the blackness of the coal mines in his native Virginia, he had spent half a lifetime in Idaho's forests.

Roark's capabilities as a hunter—he was a crack shot with an uncanny knack for spotting game—were one reason Melis wanted him to track the Ridgerunner. Roark had once helped Melis and Assistant Forest Supervisor David Kyle drag two elk out of the brushy hills near Bungalow Ranger Station, and Melis remembered Roark's effort.

At precisely 8 a.m. the morning after Cole and Holt surprised the Ridgerunner, Melis called the Forest Service warehouse in Pierce. Roark and co-worker Mickey Durant, who were repairing gear in the warehouse, had just arrived for work. Roark answered the call.

"Moton, this is Percy Melis calling from Orofino," Melis began. "Clyde Cole and Louis Holt surprised the Ridgerunner in the Flat Creek Cabin last night. They didn't arrest him because they didn't know they had the authority. I've checked with Sheriff Jack Conard; he doesn't have any deputies to spare right now, but he says we can apprehend the man. Would you go into the woods and see if you can track him down?"

"You know I will," Roark said.

"Good. Is anyone there with you?"

"Mickey Durant is here."

"You and Mickey take a truck to the Bungalow. You'll meet Cole and Holt there. They are coming out to the Bungalow from Flat Creek this morning and will bring your truck back to Pierce.

"Go down the river and pick up the Ridgerunner's trail at Flat Creek. Stay on his trail as long as you think there's a chance you can catch him, but be careful."

"We surely will," Roark replied. "Did Cole and Holt get a good look at him?"

"No. There wasn't much light in the cabin, but they could see that he is a small man. Because he's short, they thought he might be "Baldy" Weber, the escaped murderer, but they couldn't tell for sure. He had a rifle, though, and he got out of the cabin as quickly as he could. He mumbled something about having to take care of some horses. He didn't have any horses, of course. That's all that he said. Good luck."

It took Roark and Durant several hours to reach Bungalow Ranger Station. They were the first to take a vehicle over the road that year, and they had to saw through several fallen trees that blocked the way. It was late in the day by the time they turned their truck over to Holt and Cole. They spent the night at the Bungalow.

Roark and Durant set off for the Flat Creek Cabin at daybreak. Roark was certain the Ridgerunner would not return so soon to the spot where Holt and Cole surprised him, but he suspected the man might be watching the trail in case he were being pursued.

The fire of 1919 had denuded the mountains near the Bungalow. Close-packed brush grew where timber once stood; it could conceal a man easily, but Roark and Durant arrived at Flat Creek at 10 a.m. without incident.

Tracks led down the river from Flat Creek, and Roark and Durant followed them. The Ridgerunner had stayed on the trail, which surprised Roark. Maybe the man was confident that he could outdistance Holt and Cole.

Roark and Durant followed the prints for 13 miles to Canyon and on down the road from the ranger station. The tracks led past the bridge across the North Fork of the Clearwater; they stayed on the river's north side, but left the trail a short disance from the bridge.

The tracks cut over to the river bank. Roark and Durant followed them and found potato peelings on a small beach where the Ridgerunner apparently had stopped to eat. An impression in the sand marked where he had sat.

Roark and Durant could follow him no farther. Boulders lined the river bank, and Roark suspected the man had hopped from one boulder to another to leave no footprints.

For the rest of the day, Roark and Durant searched for the Ridgerunner's trail. They ranged far down the river, looking for footprints near the water's edge and on the hillsides nearby.

As they walked back to Canyon at nightfall, Roark told Durant he planned to comb the hillsides again the next day.

"If we get on his tracks, we'll stay on them no matter how long it takes."

The two men slept at Canyon and were up early to resume their search, but they went no farther than the hundred feet from the ranger station door to the trail. A new set of prints, apparently made while Roark and Durant slept, marked the trail. They were different than the prints Roark and Durant had followed the day before. Those tracks had been made by a pair of rubber boots; flat-soled boots had made the prints they saw now.

"He's changed his shoes," Roark said. "He's trying to throw us off his trail."

Roark and Durant shucked their packs. Without them, they could walk at maximum speed as they hiked up the river trail.

Six miles east of the ranger station, the tracks led up Skull Creek. Roark and Durant, their hearts pounding from exertion and excitement, followed the tracks up the creek, walking at a rapid pace for four and a half miles until the Collins Creek Cabin came into view. The cabin sat in a compact canyon that afforded little room for a man to run; if the Ridgerunner were in the cabin, he would have a hard time eluding them.

The trail crossed a wooded flat as it approached the cabin. Visibility from the cabin was good, and Roark motioned to Durant to hide behind a tree, then ducked behind a good-sized white pine himself. The two men slipped from tree to tree, working their way across the flat to a corral that sat a short distance from the cabin. They crouched behind two adjacent corral posts.

The padlock was in place on the cabin door, but the Ridgerunner might have entered the building through the window.

Roark and Durant looked at one other. Roark nodded in the direction of the cabin, and the two men raced toward the building at full speed. They skidded to a stop in front of the cabin and flattened themselves against the wall on either side of the door. They heard nothing from inside.

"I'll look in the window," Roark whispered. "You keep the door covered."

Durant nodded.

Roark dashed to the back of the building and peered carefully through the window. He saw that the cabin was empty and walked around to the front of the building.

"Let's go in Mickey," he said. "He's not here."

As they entered the building, Roark and Durant smelled a faint odor of smoke. Roark felt the side of the stove. It was warm. Someone had been inside not long before.

"Let's check outside," Roark said.

Tracks led away from the cabin and across Skull Creek atop a fallen pine. Weeks before, the cold had cemented a crust of snow to the tree, and holes in the frozen snow marked where the Ridgerunner had stepped as he crossed the log.

"He'll be back," Roark said. "There are no cabins in the direction he's gone. As cold as it's going to be tonight, he won't sleep outside if he can spend the night in a cabin. Let's hide in the brush and wait for him to come back."

It was noon when Roark and Durant lay down in the tall, brown grass on either side of the flat. The air was cool, and the minutes ticked by slowly. A gentle wind rustled the stiff grass from time to time, but otherwise they heard no sound during the long afternoon.

The sun went down, and the cold nipped at them. At length, Durant scurried stiff-legged across the flat and flopped down beside Roark.

"I can't stand it any more, Moton," Durant said. "I'm so cold my legs are cramped up."

Durant was right. Roark's legs were cramped, too. If the Ridgerunner tried to flee from them now, they wouldn't be able to chase him. It was essential for them to be able to catch the man. They had decided they would use their rifles only in self-defense.

"Let's go in the cabin and warm up," Roark said.

Roark unlocked the cabin door. After Durant went inside, Roark put the padlock back on the door and snapped it shut. If the Ridgerunner returned, the lock had to be in place or he would know someone had been inside. After Roark locked the door, he went around to the window and climbed through.

Several times that evening, Roark thought he heard a footfall on the porch. He was fighting sleep, however, and he was unsure what he had heard.

"Am I asleep? Am I awake?" Roark asked himself. He slapped himself to make sure he hadn't dropped off. Durant snored. Finally, Roark sat up on the bed. It was pitch black outside, and he could see stars through the window.

Roark let himself out through the window. Again he hid in the grass and watched the cabin. It was so dark it was all he could do to make out the building's shape. It was also bitterly cold, and Roark had to force himself not to shake as the wind blew gently through the canyon.

For the rest of the night Roark listened for a snapping twig, a rolling rock, or any other sound that would tell him someone was coming. The creek's rushing waters would muffle many noises, and Roark had no chance of hearing the Ridgerunner unless he listened intently.

The stars faded, and dawn came with its ghostly gray light. After the sun rose, Roark decided to wake Durant.

The two men looked for food in the cabin. All they found was a box of oatmeal with mouse droppings in it; the intruder had left nothing else.

Roark sifted out the droppings and cooked a kettleful of the cereal. They had no milk for the oatmeal, but they were so hungry it did not matter.

Durant was ready to turn back, but Roark said, "Mick, I'm going to cross the creek on the log that the Ridgerunner used. You can stay here if you want, but I'm going to go see where he went."

"He could be miles from here by now," Durant said. "If we were going to follow him, we should have followed him yesterday."

"You're probably right, but I'm going to take a look anyway," Roark said.

"I'll wait here," Durant said. He sat down on the porch step.

Roark crossed Skull Creek on the log that the Ridgerunner had used the day before and saw that the Ridgerunner's tracks veered up Collins Creek, which poured into Skull Creek. He had surprisingly little trouble following the tracks and wondered whether the Ridgerunner had left them deliberately.

Roark had gone about two miles when he heard a cracking noise. He froze. He knew the noise was the sound of a dead limb being pulled from a tree.

He heard the noise again; it was coming from the other side of a small hogback ridge. Roark edged his way up the ridge on his hands and knees. He heard the cracking once more and peered down the side of the ridge. A man pulled a dry branch from a dead tree and dropped it on a pile of firewood.

The man stopped beside the pile, crimped the wood against his body with his arm, and held the pile fast as he rose. In his other hand he carried a can of water. He walked toward his camp site. It appeared that he was going to build a fire and make coffee.

Just then, from behind, Roark heard someone call his name.

Roark rolled onto his back, bringing his rifle up as he turned over. Durant walked up the ridge toward him, his boots crunching the crusted snow, oblivious to the stranger's presence. Roark mouthed the words "get down" and motioned with his hand for Durant to lie prone. Durant froze. His eyebrows shot up, then he dropped and wiggled up the side of the ridge on his stomach until he lay beside Roark.

The stranger had heard nothing; he was arranging the dry branches to build a fire.

"Mick, you came up here to catch that Ridgerunner," Roark whispered. "There he is. Go get him."

Durant stared. He looked at Roark and swallowed.

Roark was uneasy, too. He knew the stranger might hear him or Durant at any moment, and he wanted to take the man by surprise.

"Now's the time to rush him, while he's bent over building a fire," Roark whispered. "Let's get up and go."

"All right," Durant said.

"Don't make any noise," Roark said. "You rush him from the left, and I'll take him from the right. He can't handle both of us at once. Take long strides so you won't slide far if you loose your footing."

"Okay."

"Let's go," Roark said.

Roark shot to his feet and bolted down the hillside. His legs carried him faster than he thought they could. The man had not looked up. Two dozen strides still separated Roark from the stranger. Roark glanced to his side to check Durant's progress, but he did not see Durant. He shot a glance over his shoulder. Durant stood on the ridge. He had not moved a step. "Mick's staying out of this," Roark thought. "I guess he's smarter than I am."

Roark was upon the man. He braked to a stop as the stranger looked up in surprise.

"Hello," Roark said.

The man was stunned. He had a branch in each hand, and he dropped the wood as he stood.

"Hello," he said. His voice shook.

The stranger wore new jeans, a new blue and black Mackinaw, and new boots. He looked well-fed, clean, and fresh-shaven. He had not been in the woods long, and Roark knew that he was not the Ridgerunner.

"You're a long way from town," Roark said.

"Yes," the fellow said.

"What are you doing way out here?"

"I came to pan for gold."

"There isn't much water for gold-panning up here," Roark said. "Where did you come from?"

"Elk River." Elk River, a tiny logging town, was 30 miles west.

"You were in the Forest Service cabin back there, weren't you?" Roark asked.

"Yes."

"I work for the Forest Service. I was sent into the woods to find a man who has been burglarizing Forest Service cabins. You don't look like him, but I've got to take you in. I have received the sheriff's authorization to arrest anyone using the cabins."

"I understand," the man said.

"What's your name?"

"Frank Davis."

Roark searched Davis. He found $47.37 in cash in Davis' pockets, along with a key made from a metal spoon. Roark held the key up to the light against his own Forest Service key. The teeth on Davis' key matched those on the Forest Service key.

Davis told Roark that he had not spent much time in the woods, but his camp belied the story. Davis had cut poles, positioned them on the ground three feet apart, and laid boughs across the poles to make a comfortable bed. A greenhorn wouldn't have done that, Roark figured.

It was still early in the day. Roark, Durant and Davis hiked to Canyon Ranger Station, which was about 12 miles away. They ate a hearty lunch, then Roark radioed Pierce to notify the Forest Service he was on the way out of the woods with a prisoner.

The three men hiked the 14 miles from Canyon to Camp 14, a PFI logging camp south of the river. The camp wasn't in operation yet; there was too much snow for the company to begin logging. The company's rail line, however, had been cleared. A PFI speeder came down the tracks from Headquarters to meet Roark, Durant, and their prisoner.

The speeder arrived in Headquarters that evening. The whole town had turned out to see the Ridgerunner; about 150 people waited near a railroad platform where the speeder stopped.

A Clearwater County sheriff's deputy grabbed Davis by the lapel and jerked him from the speeder.

"Well, if it isn't the Ridgerunner," the deputy declared. "You don't look so hard to catch, now do you? Let's see what you've got in your pockets. Come on, turn them inside out."

The deputy hit Davis across the back of his shoulders, causing the prisoner to lose his hat and almost fall down.

"Look at that son-of-a-bitch deputy, Moton," Durant said.

"Just a minute," Roark said to the deputy. "I don't think this man is the Ridgerunner. His clothes and boots are new. He hasn't spent the winter in the mountains. Just look at him."

"He's the Ridgerunner, all right," the deputy persisted, "and he's going to pay for breaking into those cabins."

"Let Louis Hold and Clyde Cole decide," Roark said.

Roark had seen a Forest Service car coming down the hill into Headquarters. He knew from his radio call that Cole and Holt would meet him at Headquarters. As soon as the car pulled to a stop, the crowd made way for Holt and Cole, and the two men climbed up the steps of the railroad platform.

"That's not him, Moton," Cole said.

"Are you sure?" Roark asked, knowing full well that Davis was the wrong man.

"I'm positive. This man is a lot taller than the fellow we saw."

"Do you agree, Louis?" Roark asked Holt.

"This is not the man we saw at Flat Creek," Holt said.

"That's what I thought," Roark said. He turned to the deputy, and gestured toward Davis.

"He told me he was in the Collins Creek Cabin," Roark said.

"We'll take him to Orofino," the deputy said.

"I'm sorry," Roark told Davis as the crowd dispersed. "I wasn't after you."

Davis was found guilty of burglary and sentenced to serve 90 days in the county jail in Orofino.

Five

Nothing turned up missing from Forest Service buildings in the Canyon and Roundtop ranger districts during the 1944 work season. Ed Barry, the new supervisor of the Clearwater National Forest, expected that the Ridgerunner's encounter with Holt and Cole accounted for the lull in the thievery; he doubted that it would last.

In his short time on the job, Barry had spent a good deal of time talking with his staff about the Ridgerunner. He believed that the man would raid the food stores in the backwoods ranger stations and cabins as soon as the Forest Service closed them for the winter, and Barry wanted Roark to spend the winter in the mountains.

Barry knew that no one could travel through the deep snow in the Clearwater Mountains without leaving a trail of some kind; sooner or later during the winter, the thief would have to leave the high country and come down into the canyons to find game or tap the rations in the cabins. Barry reasoned that if Roark traveled the back country each day, he might come across the Ridgerunner's tracks. Under those circumstances, Barry believed Roark could catch the Ridgerunner.

Roark needed work to keep him busy, and a wildlife-management problem supplied the task. An overabundance of coyotes roamed the Canyon district, taking a heavy toll on elk calves and deer. The Idaho Fish and Game Department had offered to pay trappers $100 a month to trap coyotes, and Roark was interested. He was laid off in the winter, and his seasonal Forest Service paycheck provided only a modest income for his family; traders paid $5 apiece for coyote pelts, and the Fish and Game Department allowed its trappers to sell the skins they collected. Even though he would have to spend the winter away from home, Roark wanted another chance to catch the Ridgerunner.

Barry told Roark he could stay in Forest Service cabins and use agency food supplies; in return, Roark was to keep an eye out for the Ridgerunner.

Clearwater County Sheriff Jack Conard deputized Roark at the sheriff's office; he gave Roark a pair of handcuffs and pulled a wanted poster from the wall and laid it on his desk.

The face of "Baldy" Weber glowered up from the wanted poster. Conard neatly wrote the word "Dangerous" across Weber's face in big letters and handed the poster to Roark. Roark folded the handbill-sized poster and tucked it into the breast pocket of his coat. He wanted to be able to identify Weber if he saw him.

Roark would have company in the woods. Lee Horner, an Oregonian whose reputation for woodcraft rivaled Roark's, also signed on with the Fish and Game Department. Like Roark, Horner had a family and needed the earnings from the trapping venture. He, too, had heard much about the Ridgerunner and was itching to test his mettle against the furtive stranger.

Roark and Horner split up the trapping territory. Roark trapped east from Skull Creek all the way to Bungalow Ranger Station. Horner strung out his lines west of Skull Creek. The two men agreed to meet once a week, but notify one another immediately if either came across a sign of the Ridgerunner.

As the winter progressed, Roark and Horner trapped coyote after coyote. Their piles of skins grew high, but they did not come upon a single unexplained footprint in December and January.

On Groundhog Day, Roark and Horner met at the Flat Creek Cabin for lunch. Afterwards, they walked down the river. They were about a mile upstream from the Skull Creek Cabin when they found what they had been looking for.

Someone wearing snowshoes had come up the trail. Oblong holes made by the butt of the stranger's rifle dotted the snow next to his tracks. Horner had seen no tracks when he walked up the river that morning; the prints had to be fresh.

The stranger had tramped down the snow for several feet along either side of the trail. "It looks like he was here for a while," Roark said. "I'll bet he walked up and down the trail to keep warm while he watched up the river for us."

Roark was excited. When he and Mickey Durant had set out to catch the Ridgerunner in March, they had picked up a trail that was close to two days old. This time things were different; Roark couldn't ask for a fresher trail.

Roark and Horner usually carried their rifles slung over their shoulders, but they held the guns in their hands as they set off in pursuit of the Ridgerunner. They walked swiftly and quietly, making no noise other than the soft schussing of their snowshoes through the white, powdery snow.

Roark and Horner followed the tracks to the Skull Creek Cabin; the tracks ringed the cabin before going on down the river.

Roark whispered, "He wouldn't be in the cabin would he, Lee? He wouldn't hole up in there in the middle of the day and trap himself."

"I doubt that he's in there," Horner replied, "but we've got to find out. We don't want to go down the river and have him come up behind us."

"Let's rush the place."

"All right. Let's go."

Roark and Horner's long strides carried them across the snow swiftly. In seconds the two woodsmen stood on the porch, shoulders against either side of the door jamb, listening and ready.

The padlock was in place on the door, but the lock was unclasped. Roark and Horner never left the cabins unlocked.

Roark gingerly lifted the lock off the hasp and kicked the door open. The door banged against its hinges and came part way back.

A ticking noise came out of the dark building. Roark recognized the sound. It was the ticking of an alarm clock left in the cabin by the Forest Service.

Roark knew that the clock had to be wound every 24 hours—and neither he nor Horner had used the cabin for more than a week. Someone had been inside.

Roark leaped into the cabin. He looked about quickly. The building was empty.

Horner followed Roark inside and closed the door.

"Whew," Roark exclaimed. "This is for revenue agents, not woodsmen."

"I agree," Horner said.

"He's not here, but he's been here," Roark said. "This clock has to be wound once a day or it runs down. I haven't used it in several days."

Roark picked up the clock and tried the key on its back.

"It's wound tight," he said. "It was wound a short time ago. I'll bet the Ridgerunner used it to keep track of the time while he was here."

"I smell potatoes," Horner said, sniffing the air. He knelt beside the stove and looked behind it. "There are potato peelings and coffee grounds on the floor over here by the stove."

Roark knelt on the other side of the stove to look.

"When Durant and I tried to track the Ridgerunner last March, we found potato peelings where he stopped to eat," Roark said.

The two men sat on the beds, which were opposite each other against the cabin walls. They listened to the ticking of the alarm clock.

"What should we do, Moton?" Horner asked.

"I'll bet the Ridgerunner has gone down the river to Canyon," Roark replied. "He might need supplies, and he can get anything he needs there. It will be dark before long; let's wait until dark and try to surprise him at Canyon."

The hours passed slowly while Roark and Horner prepared for their confrontation with the Ridgerunner. The two men chopped wood, built a fire in the stove, and prepared a meal; Roark washed and dried the heavy Forest Service china they used, wiping his towel round and round the green-trimmed white plates until he could see his face in them.

Meanwhile, Horner cut a palm-sized hole in the side of a five-gallon metal paint can with a pair of tin snips. A candle inside the can cast a beam of yellow light down the trail as Roark and Horner began their trek to Canyon.

It was a clear, cold night, and their breath condensed into ice crystals and coated the shoulders of their Mackinaws with white.

"How cold do you think it is?" Roark asked.

"It's got to be zero or below," Horner replied.

A crescent moon lit the woods, and the trees cast long black shadows across the trail.

Roark and Horner moved at a fast pace. As they schussed along, Roark felt optimistic. "I don't see any way he can outdo the both of us," he said. His high hopes fled abruptly, however. The Ridgerunner's tracks played out a half mile from the cabin.

Roark and Horner looked carefully for a broken branch, an overturned stone, or a mark in the snow. Any such sign could show them the way the Ridgerunner had gone, but they found nothing; it was as if the man had disappeared into thin air.

"Where in the world did he go?" Horner wondered aloud. "He couldn't just vanish. He had to walk away from here somehow."

Again and again Roark walked up and down the trail, stooping to peer at the ground while Horner held his paint-can lamp aloft. They squatted, their hands on their knees, and stared at the unbroken white snow, but they could find no indication of the Ridgerunner's trail. They were stumped.

"Let's go on to Canyon," Roark said. "There's a radio there and we can call Pierce. Who knows? He might be there. Since he knows we're in the area, he might have gone up on the hill above the trail and walked through the timber."

"What if he's not there?"

"If he's not at Canyon, he might be at the Collins Creek Cabin. As cold as it is, he wouldn't stay outdoors. Lewis had the supplies taken out of all the other cabins last fall."

"You're probably right," Horner agreed. "I'll bet he's in that cabin right now with his feet up against the stove. Since we've lost his trail I'd better get rid of this light."

Horner blew out the candle in his paint-can lantern; he and Roark walked down the trail at a businesslike pace, reaching Canyon at 9 p.m.

The trail crossed a small creek on a footbridge just east and above the station, which sat at the foot of an open hillside above a bend in the river. Roark and Horner paused to observe the buildings.

The stars snapped in the clear night sky, and the two men could see elk on the other side of the station grounds. The animals pawed the powdery snow, trying to reach the dead grass in a pasture where the Forest Service kept horses and mules during the summer. The moonlight silhouetted the elk's graceful, long necks and slender legs; the snow muffled their pawing and kept the elk from hearing Roark and Horner.

The two woodsmen could see well enough to tell that no tracks marred the snow around the buildings and no smoke rose from the chimney of the ranger's office or the stovepipes of the cookhouse and warehouse. It appeared that the ranger station was deserted, but Roark and Horner approached the office carefully and made sure the other buildings were unoccupied before they entered. Roark checked the upstairs hurriedly; Horner made certain no one hid on the ground floor. Then Roark radioed the Pierce Ranger Station.

"We'll need a portable radio so we can keep in contact, and Horner is about out of tobacco, so send in some more," Roark told Herb Flodberg, the ranger at Pierce.

Roark smiled at Horner. Horner was not authorized to stay in the government buildings or use government food, and Roark believed that the Forest Service owed Horner something for helping keep the winter-long vigil. A little tobacco wouldn't pay that debt, but it would make an installment on it.

Flodberg answered, "I'll contact Supervisor Barry right away to let him know you've cut the Ridgerunner's trail."

Within 15 minutes Flodberg radioed back. Barry had decided a team of four rangers would walk to Canyon the next day from the railroad line at Camp 14. An air drop of supplies would be made to Roark and Horner at daybreak; the airplane that brought the supplies would fly over the mountains to patrol while Roark, Horner, and the rangers searched the forest.

The rangers would reach Canyon late the next afternoon, but Roark and Horner didn't plan to wait.

"We'll be on the way to Collins Creek as soon as the air drop is made," Roark told Flodberg. "Otherwise, the Ridgerunner might get away from us."

"The plane will be there early," Flodberg promised.

Roark signed off and turned to Horner.

"Lee, we've got a good chance of catching him," Roark said. "He could go upriver or hike out of the North Fork canyon, but either way he will have slow going and leave a trail. We'll be right behind him; besides, he won't be able to outrun that airplane."

Horner looked at the thermometer that hung outside the window of the ranger's office: It stood at 2 degrees below zero.

"If he isn't in the Collins Creek Cabin tonight he's crazy," Horner said.

The men built a fire in the icy ranger's office and sat near the stove talking in low tones; they lit no lanterns and they did not sleep.

Shortly after dawn, a Johnson Flying Service Travelaire roared over the treetops near the ranger station. Dick Johnson, a pioneer in aviation in the western mountains, was at the controls. A cargo box, dropped from 1,000 feet, plummeted from a door in the plane's fuselage; a parachute broke its fall and carried it to the ground. Roark and Horner hurried across the snow to open the box. Horner found two cans of cigarette tobacco inside and stuffed them into a shirt pocket. Roark lifted a portable radio out of the box and switched it on.

"Assistant Supervisor Kyle, do you read me," Roark asked.

"Loud and clear, Moton," David Kyle said as the plane passed overhead. "Can you read me?"

"Yes," Roark answered.

"We'll be flying over the ridgetops," Kyle continued. "If he tries to hike out, we'll see him. Ranger Lewis and party are on the way in on snowshoes. Good hunting."

"We're going to close in on him now," Horner said. "That plane is as good as having a dozen men on the ground."

Within minutes, Roark and Horner were on their way up the river trail, bound for the remote cabin where they hoped to find the Ridgerunner. The sun shone brightly on the snow-covered forest. It was still cold, but the sun made the two men forget the temperature. Their spirits were high.

They grew anxious as they approached the river trail's junction with the Skull Creek trail. They feared the Ridgerunner might have come out of the canyon and fled upriver during the night, but they found no tracks leading in that direction.

Roark and Horner turned up Skull Creek, bound for the Collins Creek Cabin. The snow in the trail was deep and powdery; it hadn't been disturbed since the last snowfall several days before, and they could walk as swiftly as they wished without making noise.

They stopped a half mile from the cabin; Roark radioed the aircraft, which he and Horner could hear buzzing over the ridgetops.

"Have you seen any sign of the Ridgerunner?" Roark asked Kyle.

"Negative. We've flown along both sides of the river canyon for 20 miles. It looks like he hasn't left the canyon. Where are you now?"

"We're near the Collins Creek Cabin. We'll reach the cabin shortly. Our radio will be off to avoid noise."

"Be careful."

The Ridgerunner would have heard the drone of the plane and would be on his guard. Roark and Horner moved stealthily. As soon as the Collins Creek Cabin came into view, the two woodsmen left the trail. They had not come across the Ridgerunner's tracks, but they suspected he had traveled cross-country rather than using the trail.

They kept their rifles ready as they worked their way across the flat that Roark and Mickey Durant had traversed 11 months before. As they neared the cabin, Roark and Horner dove behind a log. Horner poked his head up to peer over the log. He saw nothing. All he heard was his own heart pounding.

"Let's circle the cabin before we rush it," Roark suggested. "Even if he slept in the cabin, I doubt that he'd stay in there all day long. If we find tracks leading away, we'll know he slipped into the woods and follow him."

Roark moved nimbly to a nearby tree; Horner darted in the other direction. Within minutes they had circled the clearing, but they found no tracks in the three-foot-deep snow. Roark's heart sank. The Ridgerunner had not been in the cabin; he had eluded them again. Roark slumped against the wall of the building. "How do you find a man who doesn't need shelter, Lee?" he asked.

"I don't know," Horner replied.

The two men stood resting with their backs against the cabin wall. Horner rolled a cigarette and lit it. Across the draw, an overloaded tree branch dumped its burden of snow; the falling powder billowed out as it made its silent drop to the ground.

"Let's radio Canyon," Roark said. "The rangers are probably there by now, and we should let them know that we had no luck."

Ranger Roy Lewis answered Roark's call. "Come on out of the drainage," Lewis ordered. "The fellows in the airplane say there still are no tracks on the ridgetops. The Ridgerunner can't have left the river canyon. It looks like we've got him hemmed in, and we can keep him trapped by patrolling the river trail."

Lewis explained that the plane would return each day as long as it was needed. He said that he and the men with him, Rangers Byron Amsbaugh and Frank "Shorty" Meneely and crewman Louis Holt, would fan out along the river trail near Canyon, leaving Roark and Horner to patrol the trail from Canyon past Skull Creek. Lewis instructed Roark and Horner to sleep at the Skull Creek Cabin, saying he and his companions would stay at Canyon.

Discouraged and weary, Roark and Horner trudged down Skull Creek. By the time they reached the mouth of the creek, they had hiked 15 miles since morning.

For the next four days, Roark, Horner, and the four other men patrolled the trail along the river, waiting for the Ridgerunner, driven by cold and hunger, to emerge. Meanwhile, the plane swooped over the ridges. The men, however, found no sign of either the Ridgerunner or his trail. Roark urged Lewis to end the patrol and search the woods. Lewis rejected the idea.

After eating dinner the night of Feb. 7, Roark and Horner sat on their bunks and talked while rain pattered on the cabin roof. The weather had changed, and maybe their luck would, too.

"The Ridgerunner has got to be up in the hills above Skull Creek hiding out," Roark reasoned. "He must have gone up there when he shook us from his trail. There is no other place he could have gone."

"I agree," Horner said.

"We don't know for sure that he has to come out of the woods," Roark continued. "I think we're just wasting our time patrolling the river trail. What do you say we go up in the mountains and find him?"

"I'm with you," Horner replied. "He won't show himself if he thinks he will be caught. If the weather was going to freeze him out, it would have done so by now, and it's changed anyway. Besides, I'm tired of patrolling."

"I hate to go against Lewis," Roark concluded, "but I know he's wrong."

Roark and Horner rose well before dawn. They began their climb into the mountains while it was still dark; they were sure the Ridgerunner would be watching downhill, and they knew they might cross his line of fire. They hoped to get above him before daylight.

The canyon wall was so steep Roark and Horner had to drop to all fours and hold onto the vegetation to pull themselves up. Occasionally, a handful of grass or brush came loose, and one of the men slid down the hill, digging his fingertips and boots into the snow to stop his slide. By dawn they had climbed much of the way up the mountain that lay between the west side of Skull Creek and the river. The rain had stopped, but it was cloudy and cool, and they pushed on.

Their plan was simple. They would climb to the top, then crisscross the mountainside on the way down, walking the length of each ridgetop and the bottom of each draw; that way, they would leave the Ridgerunner no place to hide. They planned to stalk him as if he were a deer.

They reached the top at noon and rested momentarily, but they did not stop long. It was cool, and they were eager to start their search. They began their descent a few minutes past noon, moving one at a time to lessen the chance of being seen. In two hours they were more than half way down the mountain, but had seen nothing. Then, as Roark peered through the brush, a thin wisp of smoke slipped skyward between two tall Douglas firs. The smoke disappeared immediately, but Roark riveted his eyes to the spot and motioned frantically to Horner.

"What is it?" Horner whispered.

"Smoke." Roark mouthed the word, pointing. "I saw a trickle of smoke come up over there."

Horner peered through the trees. "I can't see it," he whispered.

"It's gone now, but I know I saw it," Roark replied. "Come on."

Roark and Horner crept down the hill. They hadn't gone far when they found tracks in the snow. It was the first time they had picked up the Ridgerunner's trail since they had lost it seven days earlier.

Whoever had made the tracks had walked up the hill and gone back down.

"Let's see where he went," Roark murmured.

Roark and Horner followed the tracks a short distance up the hill to a cedar stump, where the tracks ended. Reddish wood chips, hacked from the stump with an ax, littered the ground.

"He cut firewood from this stump," Horner whispered. "His camp must be nearby."

"It sure looks that way," Roark replied. "Come on."

Roark and Horner moved down the hill again. As they followed the man's footprints, they attempted to hear every sound and to make none themselves.

They headed toward the two trees where Roark had seen the smoke. Suddenly, through a patch of thick brush, they saw a faded green tarpaulin. The tarpaulin, sagging in the middle, was hung between the two trees.

Roark and Horner moved cautiously, pausing with each step to peer ahead, guns ready. They hid behind a big white pine 15 strides uphill from the tarpaulin. A small, smokeless fire burned on the opposite side of the tarpaulin.

The camp looked deserted. The Ridgerunner might have heard them and fled. Maybe he was in the brush, with his eye trained down the barrel of his rifle on them.

"The chances are he's over there and we just can't see him," Roark whispered. "What do you say we go?"

"Okay."

Horner rushed to the left, and Roark dashed to the right.

The two men converged on the camp quickly. As soon as they could see around the tarpaulin, a man came into view. He was bent over the fire, cooking. He was unaware of their presence.

"He is a little man," Roark thought as he charged across the snow. "He could have stood up behind the tarp, and we still wouldn't have seen him."

Suddenly, one of Horner's snowshoes caught in the branches of a fallen tree hidden in the snow. He fall hard.

Horner rolled onto his side. He tried to get up, but couldn't. His snowshoe was still caught in the branches of the downed tree. He stared at the Ridgerunner while he kicked frantically to get loose.

The little man stared back, but made no move. His eyes were jet black and flashed brightly.

Finally, Horner kicked free from the branches. He scrambled to his feet and grabbed his rifle.

"Good afternoon," he said.

At that instant, Roark reached across the fire with the barrel of his rifle and tapped the stranger on the shoulder. The man turned to face Roark, but did not stand.

"Hello," Roark said.

The stranger stared at Roark, his keen black eyes boring into Roark's. For a moment, it appeared that the fellow might be frightened, but Roark could not tell for sure.

"Hello," the stranger said. His voice was high and clear and had a hint of a southern accent. "I guess the dear rangers have been looking for me for a long time," he said.

"They surely have," Roark said.

It was 2:30 p.m., Feb. 9, 1945. The hunt for the Ridgerunner was over.

Six

As Horner came up, the little fellow looked from Roark to Horner and back again. He was dirty and disheveled and his attire was ragged. Obviously, he had been in the woods for a long time, perhaps years. He wasn't "Baldy" Weber, however, and he didn't appear to be dangerous. Relieved that he and Horner had not encountered Weber, Roark sank to his haunches then sat in the snow in his heavy wool pants.

"Do you have a gun?" Roark asked.

"Over there." The Ridgerunner nodded toward a small tree. A .22-caliber bolt-action rifle leaned against the tree. It was no more than 10 steps from the fire. Roark made a mental note that the Ridgerunner had not tried to reach the gun when Horner got caught in the branches of the fallen tree.

"I'll get the gun," Horner offered. He retrieved the weapon and clicked open the chamber. It was empty.

Roark surveyed the camp. A green government sleeping bag poked out of either end of the tarpaulin. It was wet. The tarpaulin, the sleeping bag, the rifle, and a few cooking utensils appeared to be the Ridgerunner's only possessions.

Roark noticed that the Ridgerunner wore canvas pants of a type woodsmen called "tin" pants. He had on a dirty blue Mackinaw, chopped off above the elbows. Cracks split the uppers of his rubber boots, and Roark and Horner could see through the holes. He wore no sox. Dishtowels covered his feet; the light cotton towels could not possibly have kept his feet warm.

"Why would anyone want to live like this?" Roark thought.

Frying meat sputtered in the stillness of the forest. The Ridgerunner did not return to his cooking, but continued to look from Roark to Horner. Roark urged him to finish his meal.

"You must be hungry," Roark said. "Go ahead and eat. We have plenty of time."

Roark and Horner watched, fascinated, as the little man finished frying a single slice of canned corned beef and cooked three small hotcakes. The corned beef and hotcakes were the last morsels of food in his camp. His hands were steady as he soaked up the grease from his six-inch frying pan with the last bit of hotcake. He put the hotcake in his mouth and set the pan aside.

The stranger was not a handsome man. He had a narrow, almost pinched face, and his nose turned up. He was approaching middle age, if not already there. His hair and beard were trimmed, though unruly. To Roark, he looked more pitiable than fearsome.

"We found a track and wondered who in the world it could be," Roark said. "How about coming down to our cabin with us?"

The little man gave Roark a hard look, but said nothing.

"We're hungry and we want something to eat," Roark persisted. "We've been walking all day. Come with us and we'll all have a good dinner."

Either the stranger's doubts eased or he saw he had no choice but to accompany Roark and Horner. "I'll take this sleeping bag back," he offered. "That's where I got it, down at the cabin. I'll take it back."

Roark didn't want the Ridgerunner to worry about the worn sleeping bag.

"The government has a lot of sleeping bags," he replied. He added, "I'm going to have to search you."

The Ridgerunner stood to his full height—five feet, two and one-quarter inches—and stretched his arms away from his 130-pound frame, indicating his consent to be searched. In his pockets he carried a jackknife, fishing line, bottles of boric acid and oil of cloves, and a plastic sack of .22-caliber cartridges. Around his neck, tucked into a small Bull Durham tobacco pouch, was a key made from a corned beef tin. Inserted into a Forest Service lock alongside the jackknife's thin blade, it worked perfectly.

"What's your name?" Roark asked.

"Bill Moreland," the little man replied.

"Do you have any identification?"

"No."

"Not even a Social Security card?"

"What's that?"

"It's a card that shows you're signed up for a government pension program. Every working person has to have one. When you sign up, they give you a number. It's on the card."

"I've never heard of Social Security. When did the government start it?"

"In 1935."

"I haven't had a job since then."

"Oh."

It seemed odd to Roark that Moreland hadn't heard of Social Security, but he decided to drop the matter. He knew Lewis would want to know that the Ridgerunner was in custody, and he wanted to get moving.

"We can talk more later," Roark said. "We'd better start down the mountain before it gets late. You walk between us. We won't hurt you. Don't try to run away."

"I won't," Moreland promised.

Horner carried the little man's sleeping bag, and Roark packed Moreland's rifle as they set off for the Skull Creek Cabin, leaving the worn tarpaulin behind. The woods were quiet as Roark, Horner, and Moreland hiked along. Soon they could see the river. They stopped to rest where they had a good view across the canyon; under the gray late-afternoon sky, the timber on the faraway slopes took on a deep blue color. The three men stood quietly, breathing deeply and resting.

"Did dear old Franklin D. get elected again?" Moreland asked.

"Yes, he did," Horner said.

"I figured he would. I saw some newspapers in the lookouts that said he was running."

A raven, his presence betrayed by a backdrop of white snow, flew between stands of trees on the other side of the river.

"You fellows aren't rangers, but there are rangers with you, aren't there?" the Ridgerunner asked.

"Yes," Roark replied.

"Is one of them Roy Lewis?"

"Yes. How did you know his name?"

"I've seen him on the trail lots of times. He runs the Canyon."

"That's right." Roark knew that Lewis had never seen the Ridgerunner before.

"Was Lewis in that contemptible airplane?"

"No. He's been patrolling the trail near the ranger station with three other men."

"I would have left days ago if it hadn't been for that airplane."

Horner had been dying to know how the Ridgerunner had eluded him and Roark.

"We tried to follow you down by the river after we found your tracks," Horner said. "How did you shake us?"

"You know that little trickle of water that runs across the trail about a half mile from the Skull Creek Cabin?"

"Yes. It's right where we lost your tracks. I threw a cigarette butt into it while we tried to figure out which way you went."

"I stepped off the trail into that trickle and walked up the hill."

"But it wasn't as wide as the sole of a boot."

"Yes it was—just. I was careful not to slip and leave a mark in the snow. I figured you would never guess I could walk in such a small amount of water."

"You figured right."

Roark also had a question for the Ridgerunner.

"Would you have holed up much longer where we found you?" he asked.

"No. I had to move because I was out of food. I was going to move early tomorrow."

"Do you travel in the daytime, usually?"

"I travel mostly at night. The game moves at night, so that's when I move. If somebody is out on the trail, they spook the game, and I hear them." The tactic made sense.

The three men rested for a few more minutes, then headed down the mountain, reaching the Skull Creek Cabin at 4 p.m. Roark loaded his arms with firewood from a pile outside, and they went into the building. As Roark and Horner went about their business, they continued to talk easily with the stranger; in truth, they had more in common with him than they did with the college-educated rangers.

Like Moreland, Roark and Horner thought nothing of spending weeks alone in the mountains. They knew that many men who lived in the forest had reasons for seeking solitude, and they did not press Moreland with questions. Roark gave Moreland a pair of wool socks; the little man accepted the socks eagerly, removed the dish towels from his feet, and pulled the socks on.

During dinner, Roark thought long and hard about how to let Lewis know that the Ridgerunner was in custody. He didn't want to alarm

Moreland, but he had to contact Lewis. Finally, Moreland gave him the answer to the dilemma.

"What's that?" Moreland asked, pointing at the radio that the airplane had dropped to Roark and Horner.

"It's a radio," Roark explained. "I'll show you how it works."

"They have one of those at Canyon," Moreland continued. "I tried every dial on the dear thing, but couldn't get it to work."

"Maybe the batteries were dead," Roark said.

Roark switched the set on.

"Skull Creek calling Canyon," he said.

"Skull Creek, this is Canyon," came the reply.

The Ridgerunner shot out of his chair, strode across the room, and peered into the receiver.

"This is Moton Roark," Roark responded. "Can you have beds ready for three men tonight? Two of us went out today, and three of us are coming back."

"That's affirmative." Roark recognized Byron Amsbaugh's voice, and Amsbaugh was excited.

"We will be leaving soon," Roark added.

A different voice came over the radio, and Roark recognized it as Lewis's.

"Ranger Meneely and I will walk up the trail to meet you," Lewis said.

"We'll see you along the river," Roark replied.

"Skull Creek clear."

"Canyon clear."

Roark switched off the set. The rangers knew what they needed to know, and Roark didn't want persistent calls from them to dampen Moreland's spirits. The little man, however, seemed unbothered by the rangers' interest in his capture.

Roark wanted to know one more thing. He had been surprised to learn that Moreland hadn't heard of Social Security; Moreland's unfamiliarity with radios also seemed strange.

"How long have you been in the woods?" Roark asked.

"Since the first time Franklin D. ran for election."

"That was 1932! That was 13 years ago."

"Is it 1945?" Moreland said. "I'm 44 years old. I thought I was 43."

Roark shook his head. The Ridgerunner was so out of touch that he didn't know what year it was.

The men continued to converse as they prepared to leave. Roark and Horner felt a growing rapport with the Ridgerunner, and Roark decided to enlist Moreland's help in a practical joke. Frank Meneely, one of the rangers who would be coming up the trail, constantly pulled tricks on Roark, and Roark saw an opportunity to get even with him.

"When we meet the rangers, act like the short one is an old pal," Roark told the Ridgerunner. "It will be easy for you to tell him from Lewis. Lewis is tall, and you know what he looks like. The little fellow's name is Frank Meneely, and his nickname is 'Shorty.'"

Horner laughed aloud, but the Ridgerunner was cool to the idea.

"You're just trying to get this Shorty fired," he said.

"No we're not," Roark protested. "He's pulled a hundred tricks on me."

"I'll go you one better," the Ridgerunner promised.

Moreland walked between Roark and Horner as the three men hiked down the narrow trail to Canyon, but took the lead when they saw the ranger's flashlights approaching. Lewis and Meneely ached with curiosity to see the Ridgerunner and were surprised that he was leading Roark and Horner down the trail; without breaking stride, he walked up to Meneely and extended his hand.

"Hello, Shorty," he said. "I'm glad to see you again. I wanted to return those salmon eggs I borrowed last summer when we were fishing together up the river, but I left the eggs in camp."

The startled Meneely jerked his hand away.

"I don't know you and I don't know anything about any salmon eggs," he exclaimed.

Roark and Horner exploded with laughter; Meneely realized that he had been had.

"Darn you guys," he said.

The sheepish Meneely held out his hand to Moreland a second time. "I've wanted to meet you for a long time," he said.

"Proud to know you," Moreland replied.

"What is your name?" Meneely asked.

"They call me Moreland," the little man said. To Meneely, Moreland's slight drawl made the name sound like "Morl'n."

Lewis also shook hands with the Ridgerunner, but he was not as cordial as Meneely.

"Let's go," the ranger said brusquely. "I'll lead, Frank. You follow me. Moreland will come next, then Roark and Horner."

When the woodsmen and their prisoner entered the Canyon Ranger Station office, Amsbaugh and Holt stared at Moreland even after introductions were made. Meneely and Lewis also watched intently as Moreland took off his brimless, visor-less hat, which he had made from a scrap of gray wool blanket. He also removed his Navy blue Mackinaw, which was shy of buttons. Underneath the Mackinaw, he wore a remnant of drab green Forest Service blanket. The poncho-like garment was open on the sides and hung down to his knees. He had made it by cutting a hole in the center for his head and apparently wore it for warmth. The other men couldn't help but notice how dirty the wet woolen items were; they smelled of must and smoke.

The Ridgerunner wore a brown checked wool shirt; he had chopped the sleeves off at the elbow, and the arms of a sweater protruded from under the shirt's sleeves. Lewis recognized the sweater as one of his wife's. He recalled that it had turned up missing from the ranger's residence at Canyon. It troubled him to see the Ridgerunner in his wife's sweater, but he said nothing.

Moreland sat down, stretching his arms along the arms of his chair. The other men could see that his small hands were hard and rough. His rubber boots, which had calks in the instep, looked to be several sizes too large and had no laces.

"What kind of camp did he have?" Lewis asked Roark.

"He was using a tarp thrown over a rope for shelter," Roark said. "He was camped near a small creek which had come up when it rained, getting his sleeping bag wet. He had a little fire going when we found him."

"Was he up on the hill about where you thought he'd be?"

"Yes."

The Ridgerunner sat stoically while the other men talked about his capture.

"Did he have any equipment with him?" Lewis asked.

"He had a kapok sleeping bag and a blanket from the Skull Creek Cabin," Roark replied. "He had a hatchet, a flashlight, and a bottle of oil with a wick in it. He also had a .22 rifle and a handful of shells."

"There were some salmon eggs in his camp," Horner volunteered.

The Ridgerunner, Roark, and Meneely smiled at Horner's comment.

"How did you find him?" Lewis asked.

"We climbed to the top of the ridge between Nub Creek and Skull Creek, then 'contoured' back down until we cut his track near his camp." By "contoured," Roark meant that he and Horner had walked back and forth across the mountain as they dropped to lower elevations; contour lines on a map run back and forth to indicate changes in elevation.

"He had gone uphill after firewood and walked back down," Roark continued. "We saw smoke and rushed him."

"Did he offer resistance?"

"No."

Lewis asked Meneely and Amsbaugh to take notes while he asked questions.

"Let's start at the beginning," Lewis said to the Ridgerunner. "For the record, what's your full name?"

"I've used several names, but I was born under the name W.C. Morrison," the little man replied.

"Do you have any nicknames?"

"I've been called Wildcat from being in the brush so much when I was young."

"Where were you born?"

"Wolfe County, Kentucky."

"Were you born in a town?"

"No."

"Where do you live?"

"In the woods."

"Do you have a residence with an address?"

"No. I move too much."

"Where do you vote?"

"I've never voted in my life."

The Ridgerunner believed that his father was still alive and lived in Morgan County, Kentucky. He said he had received a letter from his father during World War I, but his mother was dead and he had not heard from his sister in 25 years.

"Have you ever been in the armed forces?" Lewis asked.

"I tried to get in the Army during World War I at Esconobic, Michigan, but I was too young to go to war and there was something wrong with my arches."

Moreland's answer made Lewis pause. Moreland could travel through the forest well enough to elude Roark, but claimed to have bad arches. Lewis hadn't anticipated that, and he was surprised by something else. He had suspected that the Ridgerunner was a mental incompetent, but the little man's flashing black eyes indicated keen intelligence.

"Have you ever been fingerprinted?" Lewis asked.

"They took my prints 14 years ago when a railroad agent took me off a freight at Seattle," Moreland answered. "I was fingerprinted when I was taken off a freight at Tacoma, too. They've got my prints at the Arizona State Prison at Florence and the Tupper Farm of the Arkansas State Prison."

"You've been in prison in Arizona and Arkansas?"

"Yes."

"Why were you in prison in Arizona?"

"I didn't have a key to the door of the grocery store and I needed something to eat, so I tore the door down."

It was obvious Moreland was making an attempt at humor, and the other men smiled.

He said he was sentenced to one to three years in the case, but was an innocent bystander when he was imprisoned in Arkansas.

"There was a 10-cent bank robbery," he contended. "I wasn't concerned nor participating. I stole a horse to avoid questioning. I got caught with the horse."

He said he served two years in prison in Arkansas and then was released.

"You said you were taken off a freight in Tacoma," Lewis asked. "When were you in Tacoma?"

"Fifteen years ago, approximately."

"Did you look for work there?"

"I took all the jobs I could get. I washed dishes mostly."

"When did you first come into the forest?"

"I believe it was about 12 years ago. F.D.R. had served one year of his first term."

"That would have been 1933?" Lewis asked.

"Actually, I think I went into the woods in 1932."

"And you've been there ever since?"

"Yes."

The Forest Service men looked at one other in disbelief. Thirteen years was an incredibly long time to live in the forest as Moreland had lived.

"What was your intention in coming to the woods?" Lewis asked.

"I wanted to live like a coyote, just live from day to day."

"Did you have any partners?"

"No."

"Not at any time?"

Moreland shook his head.

"Did you know Frank Davis?" Davis was the man whom Roark and Mickey Durant had apprehended in the woods the previous spring.

"Never heard of him," Moreland said.

"Did you take any ration books from the ranger station?"

"I never heard of them, either," Moreland said.

"They're for commodities that are being rationed because of the war effort," Lewis explained.

"I don't need them," Moreland said. "I get my grub from the government cabins."

"How do you get into the cabins?"

"I use a key. I have a key to both the front door and the back door of this building. The radio here fooled me. I thought it was a dictaphone. I would have taken it, but I couldn't get it to work."

"Have you spent most of your time in Idaho?"

"Yes."

Moreland claimed that he had been in the hills near Hamilton, Montana, and stayed at Powell Ranger Station several times. Hamilton, a small town, was on the east side of the Bitterroot Mountains, and Powell was 25 miles away on the west side. It was 110 miles from Canyon to Powell via trails and roads that crossed a steep, rugged divide separating the North Fork and the Lochsa River. The name of the latter stream, pronounced "Lock-saw," was derived from a Flathead Indian word for "rough water." The word aptly described the turbulent stream.

"Where did you get your rifle?" Lewis asked.

"I borrowed it from the Skull Creek Cabin two years ago," Moreland replied. "I went there to get some food, and when I found the rifle I got so excited I ran out and forgot all about the food."

"What about your clothes?"

"I picked them up in the camps."

"What towns did you visit when you needed things?"

"I didn't go to any towns."

"You mean in 13 years you were never in a town?"

"No. I never did make contact with the outside. The best places to find things were the ranger stations and lumber camps."

If Moreland had lived as he claimed, he had experienced near total isolation for more than a decade.

Lewis picked up the questioning.

"Where did you get your snowshoes?" he asked.

"I'm not certain. I made my first pair. I took this pair from either Camp T or the Diamond Match Camp. They were left hanging on some wire between two trees in the summer time."

"Where did you get the clothing you're wearing?" Lewis asked.

"I got my pants and boots from Camp P last fall. A fellow was there taking things with a packsack when I arrived. There was lots of peanut butter in the back room." Camp P was another PFI camp.

"Do you have any caches?" Lewis asked.

"I have clothes hidden in several places, but the 'geesely' federals kept destroying my caches. They drove nails into the cans of food."

The other men were unfamiliar with the word "geesely." They were unsure what it meant, but realized Moreland used it as an insult. Moreland's comment irritated Lewis.

"I don't believe that anyone bothered your caches," Lewis snapped. "In fact, I'll bet you don't have any caches."

"I have a cache out here in the front yard," Moreland declared.

"Show us."

"All right."

The little man rose and walked out the door with Lewis behind him. Roark followed, carrying a Coleman lantern; he, Horner, Meneely, Amsbaugh, and Holt trailed Moreland and Lewis to a corner of the clearing in front of the ranger's office.

The Ridgerunner walked to a large rock that sat at the edge of the station pasture. He stooped and began digging under the rock with his bare hands. He had no gloves, but the snow didn't seem to bother him. Lewis knelt beside Moreland to watch, and Roark held the lantern high to provide light. The hardened snow crunched under the other woodsmen's boots as they shifted their weight while Moreland dug. At length, Moreland pulled a small, worn burlap sack from under the rock and handed it to Lewis.

"Here," he said.

The ranger unrolled the sack and opened it. He reached inside and found a fishing line wrapped around a wood chip and held fast by a rusty fishhook. Lewis also found three tins of meat and a pair of pants that were several sizes too large for Moreland.

"I think I recognize these," Lewis said. "Let's go back inside."

While the other men sat down, Lewis picked up a chunk of split cedar from the woodbox near the door. He opened the stove and shoved the wood inside. The light from the stove's open door sent shadows along the walls. It was warm in the little building; Lewis set the pants on the edge of his desk.

"Where did you get these?" he asked. He leaned back in his chair and clasped his hands behind his head. Moreland looked carefully at the pants.

"I got them in one of the lumber camps," he answered. He pulled a corncob pipe from the breast pocket of his shirt and filled it with tobacco from a bag Horner had given him.

"I lost a pair of pants just like these," Lewis said. He leaned forward, picked up the trousers and began to unroll them. "Do you know what happened to my pants? They were at my house here at Canyon the last time I saw them."

"I took your pants, but they were too long," the Ridgerunner answered, holding a match to his pipe. He puffed to make the tobacco catch, then held his hands about a foot apart and added, "I cut about this much off the legs so they would fit."

The other men fought to suppress their grins, but Lewis saw no humor in Moreland's remark.

"I suppose the pants aren't much good now," he said. "Did you wear them out?"

"No," Moreland replied. "They're hidden on the other side of the river. They didn't fit even after I sawed them off so I didn't wear them."

The other men knew that Moreland's thievery had put a tremendous strain on Lewis, and they weren't surprised by Lewis' cool tone.

"Did you find any money while you were going through the cabins and lumber camps?" he said.

"I found $3.10 in the pocket of W.C. Turner's pants," Moreland answered. "Turner should have seen me. He looked right at me."

Lewis asked him whether he could read maps.

"I've had lots of experience reading maps," Moreland replied. "I took maps as I needed them. I can draw better maps than the Forest Service."

"You can draw better maps than the Forest Service?"

"Yes. The Forest Service maps are wrong about some things. The Forest Service has Eagle Point four drainages over from the Canyon. It's three drainages over."

"I'm sure the Forest Service maps are right," Lewis said.

"He's right about that, Roy," Meneely interjected. "Our maps do have Eagle Point mislabeled."

Lewis changed the subject.

"Have you had your key for a long time?" he asked.

"Yes. I made it at Elbow Bend Ranger Station over in the Selway."

"Where did you get the pattern for your key?"

"Someone left a key in a lock by mistake. I made an impression of it in a bar of soap and then made my own key from the impression. I tried my key a dozen times before it finally worked at Deep Creek while I was still in the Selway."

"Is this the same key you've had all along?"

"No. My key broke occasionally, and I made a new one from a tobacco can. I've seen keys made."

Lewis asked Moreland whether he was glad he had been caught.

"I'm proud they found me," Moreland responded. "It was getting tiresome."

"I sure didn't like the candle grease on the floors of the buildings."

"I didn't use candles here at the station. I used a bottle with a lamp wick in it. This is at my camp now. I used candles elsewhere, and I took all of them I found in the cabins so no one could follow me in the dark. I hid two candles under the mattress at Skull Creek."

"What appealed to you in the Canyon country?"

"The good cabins and rough mountains."

"Did you have any way to keep track of time?"

"No. I thought it was March of 1944. By June 15 the Goat Ridge Lookout generally is occupied."

"Where did you stay last summer?"

"I was near Camp W most all summer. Once I had to wait around for two days while a man was getting ready to leave." PFI's Camp W was on the opposite side of the river from Canyon.

Moreland had spent part of the winter at Gold Hill, which was west of the Canyon district. He also had stayed at Skull Creek for two weeks, spending three nights in the cabin.

"Where did you stay the winter before?" Lewis asked.

"At Roundtop. I had a camp about one mile from the ranger station. The federals just about got me there."

Lewis assumed that Moreland was referring to his footrace with Merrill Oaks.

"Did you ever have a pair of binoculars?" Lewis asked.

"Yes."

"Where did you get them?"

"I got them at Roundtop and left them at the Collins Cabin. I got a radio one time from Roundtop, but someone found the cache it was in and took it."

Lewis listened intently. He knew that the binoculars found at the Collins Creek Cabin came from Roundtop—and that a radio had been stolen from there.

Moreland had visited Boston Mountain, where he found some eggs in a cabin and cooked them, and Salmon Mountain. He also had been to Square Top, where he saw a cougar. The rangers recognized the names of the three mountains, which were between the Selway River and the Salmon River. Moreland had worked his way north through Idaho in his travels.

Moreland also claimed he had passed by an Indian village where he sprang two traps so animals wouldn't get caught in them; the rangers suspected he had skirted an encampment that Nez Perce Indians put up periodically near the Salmon River.

"Where have you held a job?" Lewis asked.

"I worked at Iron Mountain, Michigan," Moreland said. "I got put in jail there. I worked in camp No. 12, No. 10 and No. 30."

"When did you leave Michigan?"

"Twenty-five years ago."

It was getting late, and Lewis decided to call a halt to the questioning.

Moreland seemed undisturbed when Lewis told him he would be taken to town the next day. Still, Lewis was concerned that Moreland might try to escape during the night. He instructed Meneely and Amsbaugh to take the Ridgerunner upstairs to sleep and put their beds under the windows on either end of the attic. "If he tries to get away, he'll have to climb over one of you," Lewis said.

After the three men went upstairs, Lewis closed the door to the stairs and blocked it with his own bed.

The night passed uneventfully. Even though Meneely and Amsbaugh were in the same room with a man who had been sought for years, they slept soundly. Moreland made no sound until morning.

SEVEN

When Meneely came downstairs the next morning, he found the Ridgerunner in the kitchen surveying the contents of the cupboard.

"What are you looking for?" Meneely asked.

"I'm not sure," the Ridgerunner said, "I've been here so many times it didn't seem right to leave without taking something."

Meneely burst out laughing.

Roark talked privately with Moreland as the others prepared to leave.

"Horner and I are going to stay in the mountains another month," Roark explained. "I know they're going to put you in jail when they get you to town. When we come out of the woods, I'll visit you. Meantime, is there anything I can do for you?"

"Yes, there is," Moreland replied. "I've got another cache under the front porch. Would you hide it so they don't pin that on me, too?"

"I'll take care of it. By the way, did you know that Horner and I were nearby before we picked you up?"

"I knew you would be following me after I saw your tracks down by the river. I tried to throw you off by chopping down some small trees at the mouth of Skull Creek. I limbed the trees and floated them down the river; I thought you would see the stumps and think I had made a raft and crossed the river."

The gambit was a good one, even though Roark hadn't noticed the stumps. Perhaps snow had covered them.

The rangers radioed the Pierce Ranger Station to get the weather forecast. The radio operator said clear weather was expected, and the rangers asked to have a PFI speeder meet them along the company's rail line. They were worried that the Ridgerunner might make a break for it, and as they strapped on their snowshoes, Lewis devised a scheme to keep him in tow.

"You walk between Meneely and me and keep up," Lewis told Moreland. "I'll lead and Shorty will be right behind you. Stay between us, now."

The tall ranger lit out up the road as fast as his long legs would carry him. Moreland was right behind and stayed right behind. Meneely had to run to keep up.

In the afternoon, the winded Lewis relinquished the lead to Holt, who slogged through the snow as fast as he could. The Ridgerunner stayed on his heels, with Amsbaugh just a few feet behind. After an hour of keeping pace with Holt, the exhausted Moreland toppled over in the snow. Amsbaugh offered to help him up, but the little man waved Amsbaugh off and indicated that he needed a moment's rest.

"What's the matter?" Amsbaugh asked. "You've been walking on snowshoes all winter. You should be toughened up."

"I've walked a long way on snowshoes," Moreland said, "but this is the first time I've ever tried running on them."

At 2 p.m., the party arrived at Camp 14, where the rangers planned to spend the night. Darkness would overtake them long before they could reach the next shelter. Moreland had cramps in his legs and didn't feel well, but he was ready to talk when the men rolled out their sleeping bags in the log-scaler's shack. Like Roark and Horner, Meneely, Amsbaugh, and Holt were beginning to warm up to Moreland. He seemed unworried about the legal jeopardy he faced, and the three men asked him questions that went far beyond the purpose of investigation. He told them stories about his exploits, including how he stayed one step ahead of Merrill Oaks when the Roundtop ranger tried to track him.

"I saw him when he came to the woods with his search parties," Moreland explained. "I went up to a lookout and listened on the telephone while he talked to the forest supervisor about his plans."

Moreland told a story about a lumberjack whom he encountered along a log-carrying flume.

"I was walking up the Beaver Creek Flume once when I heard someone coming the other way," he said. "I jumped off the flume and hid in the brush. A lumberjack stopped nearby, took off his pack and hung it on the walkway along the flume. He must have forgotten something because he left his pack and walked back toward camp.

"As soon as he was gone, I grabbed the pack and took it into the brush to go through it, but the lumberjack came back before I was through. When he couldn't find the pack, he must have thought he left it at camp, because he walked back that way.

"While he was gone, I put the pack back on the flume. Pretty soon he came back and found it just where he had left it.

"He wouldn't touch that pack for a long time. He walked around it and cussed it. Finally, he put it on, climbed back on the flume and walked away. He didn't look inside. I had his tobacco."

Moreland's smell was inescapable in the crowded little shack, but his stories held the other men's interest, and he delighted in telling them.

"Was there a time when you thought you wouldn't make it?" Amsbaugh asked him.

"I just about starved when I came into the North Fork country," Moreland replied. "I stumbled onto a cabin on Pot Mountain or I wouldn't be here now. All there was in the cabin was peanut butter. I found it in the food cache under the floor. I was so hungry I ate it with my fingers. It kept me alive."

"Did you ever think you would be caught?" Meneely asked.

"When I was in the basement of the Goat Ridge Lookout one night the moon came up and shined through the door, which I had left open. I thought someone had put a flashlight on me, and I yelled, 'Don't shoot.' After I realized it was only the moon, I was afraid I might have woke the kid upstairs, so I got out of there."

The men ate a sparse meal of canned rations before bedding down, but Amsbaugh slept poorly. He still wondered whether Moreland was dangerous.

The cold night air cemented a hard crust atop the snow, and when the five men left Camp 14 at 7:25 a.m., they carried their snowshoes and walked atop the crust. After Moreland's ailments the day before, it was evident there was no need to tire him, and Lewis set a modest pace. The rangers followed the PFI rail line to Camp 6, which was nine miles from Camp 14, and stopped to brew coffee. The hot liquid warmed their insides. Moreland sipped a cup, but said little during the half-hour break. The crust gave out at Camp 6, and the five men put on their snowshoes. At 1:35 p.m. they arrived at Murphy Siding, which was six miles from

Headquarters. They walked down the tracks another mile and a half before the PFI speeder came.

Eleven men had ridden down the tracks from Headquarters in the yellow, gasoline-powered speeder, taking up all but the five seats that the Forest Service men and Moreland would occupy. The speeder pulled a trailer carrying another dozen men, who were warmed by curiosity despite their open-air ride.

The other passengers said little to the Ridgerunner during the short ride to Headquarters, but they stared at him all the way. Moreland ignored their gazes. The speeder arrived in Headquarters at 3 p.m. Once again, the whole town turned out to see the Ridgerunner, but Moreland was whisked from the speeder to a waiting government car, which left immediately. He was not handcuffed.

The rangers stopped at Pierce for dinner, then continued on to Orofino, arriving at 6:05 p.m. When Moreland stepped out of the car in front of the Clearwater County Courthouse, David Kyle was struck by how dirty he was.

"He's so dirty his skin is shiny," the assistant forest supervisor thought. "I'll bet the dirt won't stick to him anymore. He must not have had a bath in years."

A photographer snapped pictures of Moreland standing between two strapping six-foot officials. One of the pictures ran the next morning in *The Spokesman-Review,* Spokane's morning daily newspaper, under a banner headline that said, "Phantom Fugitive of Forest Caught at Last."

That week's edition of Orofino's weekly paper, *The Clearwater Tribune,* reported that Moreland's apprehension ended "one of the Northwest's most persistent manhunts." According to the paper, Moreland snapped, "I'm guilty as hell."

Sheriff Conard fingerprinted Moreland at his office counter near the sturdy doors of the Clearwater County Jail, which were made from a lattice of wide, flat, steel bars.

FBI agent Ed Mayer and law enforcement officer A.J. "Bert" Cramer of the Forest Service were waiting at the sheriff's office to interview Moreland. Kyle, Lewis, and Meneely listened during the interview.

Moreland told Mayer that he was born on Oct. 1, 1900, near Landsaw, Kentucky, and that his full name was William C. Moreland. He said his father's name was W.L. Moreland and that his mother's maiden name was Emmie Stone. He had a sister named Stella, but didn't know whether he was older or younger than her.

"You don't know whether you are older or younger than your sister?" Mayer asked.

"My parents separated when I was small," Moreland said. "My father took my sister and my mother took me."

After his mother died when he was nine or ten, Moreland went to live with his grandmother on a farm near Indiana. Her name was Corrie Stone. From his grandmother's home, he was sent to live in Covington, Kentucky.

"Did you go to school there?" Mayer asked.

"I went to school to about the fifth grade."

"Why did you stop attending school?"

"Because I was sent to reform school. I ran away from the people I stayed with in Covington."

Moreland was in the reform school for about a month, then ran away again.

"Then what happened?" Mayer asked.

"I was picked up and put in another reform school."

"And?"

"I ran away again and was picked up again."

"How long did this go on?"

"For some time. I kept running away from the schools, and each time the railroad police picked me up."

He went to his first reform school when he was 12, and he was in the places until he was 16, Moreland claimed.

"I recall being in reform schools in Lancaster, Ohio, and in the states of Kentucky, Michigan, Wisconsin, Texas, and a few others," Moreland said. "I was picked up a few times in Oklahoma."

When he left reform school for the last time, Moreland went to work for a lumber company in Michigan, then went to Sault Ste. Marie and worked on an ore boat.

"I finally reached Pennsylvania, where I stowed away on a McCormick Steamship Co. boat which took to sea," he said. "I was not discovered until we were somewhere off the New Jersey coast. They put me to work washing dishes."

Moreland was unsure where the freighter sailed, but after three months at sea it landed in Seattle.

"What year was this?" Mayer asked.

"I'm not sure. The first World War was over when we landed."

"What did you do in Seattle?"

"I washed dishes in restaurants and on a Coast Guard boat. I lived between two bridges near a sawmill in Tacoma. I think this was about the time Hoover was president. Times were tough and I could get only 25 cents for unloading a full truckload of wood."

Moreland headed south to Vancouver, Washington, then to a place called Washam, then to Bend, Oregon, "where I bummed around town for 8 to 10 days." From Bend, Moreland went to another town, the name of which he couldn't remember, then back to Washam, and on to Pendleton, Oregon. He thought he went to Pasco next, then to Umatilla, Oregon, and Lewiston, Idaho.

"There was very little work," Moreland remembered. "I drifted like this for about four years."

"Did you find any work at all in that time?"

"Yes. I hired out, in Lewiston I think, to a sheepman who took me to a place on the Snake River near Mountain Home. He had a little farm, and I did the irrigating and skinned some sheep for him."

"What year was this?"

"This was about the time Roosevelt was first getting elected. During the time I was on this ranch I was told the bank at Mountain Home had been robbed. I stayed at this place for about six weeks."

Moreland told Mayer about his stints in prison in Arkansas and Arizona.

"What did you do after getting out of prison?" the FBI agent asked.

"I bummed around the country a lot. I never held any job for any length of time, just did odd jobs and once in a while some farm work. I used to try to bum the chain gangs in Louisiana for food."

Mountain Home was the last town of any size he was in before he went into the mountains, Moreland said.

"Ranger Lewis tells me that you haven't been to a town in 13 years. Is that right?" Mayer asked.

"Yes."

"You mean that you never went to a town for any reason after you left Mountain Home?"

"Well, right after I left Mountain Home, I stopped at a mining town, bought some tobacco and started traveling in the mountains."

"What was the name of the mining town?"

"I don't know."

"What direction were you headed?"

"North."

Meneely interrupted. "It was probably Atlanta," he said.

"Thanks," Mayer replied, turning again to Moreland. "How did you find your way through the mountains?"

"I had some maps that I got at Avery. As I remember, I got off a freight there and saw a cabin. I went in, ate some food, picked up the maps, took a shirt off the line, and left."

It was late in the summer when he went into the mountains, Moreland explained. He said he spent the first winter in the Sawtooths, living mostly on venison. "I might have spent two winters in this area," he added.

The Sawtooth Mountains were 300 miles south of the Canyon Ranger District. They were high, jagged mountains and even more inhospitable than the Clearwater range.

Moreland then went to Shoup, Gibbonsville, and the Chamberlain Basin. His destinations were more than 70 air miles from the Sawtooth Mountains, where he spent his first winter. The Chamberlain Basin, where hundreds of elk from the Salmon River's herds give birth each spring, was halfway back across Idaho from Gibbonsville. Moreland said that he reached the Chamberlain Basin in June.

"I tried to steal an airplane there, but I couldn't get it started," he said. "I found keys in the plane and turned everything on, but it wouldn't start."

"Do you know how to fly a plane?" Mayer asked.

"No."

Moreland's attempt at aviation baffled his listeners, but Mayer didn't pursue the matter. He had plenty of other questions to ask.

After leaving the Chamberlain Basin, Moreland roamed the Salmon River country, working his way up and down the river, then ranged north to the Selway River by way of the tiny towns of Dixie and Elk City and the Meadow Creek Ranger Station.

"Did you encounter anyone during this time?" Mayer asked.

"I almost got caught near Meadow Creek when I set my packsack down and left it. When I came back someone had picked it up and left his own packsack, which I took."

Moreland's listeners couldn't help but wonder whether he was responsible for any switching of packs that occurred.

From Meadow Creek, Moreland had gone to Deep Creek Ranger Station, then back to Meadow Creek. He said that he spent more than a year moving around the Selway country and was in Forest Service ranger stations, cabins, or lookouts at Meadow Creek, Deep Creek, Bear Creek, Sixty-Two, Rhoda Creek, and Fish Lake.

The Selway country was rocky and hot and a haven for rattlesnakes. Almost totally undeveloped, it was to become one of the country's first federally designated wilderness areas, and the swift, pristine Selway River was to become one of America's first federally designated wild rivers.

"Did you have a key to Forest Service locks while you were in the Selway area?" Mayer asked Moreland.

"I had a homemade key, but I also made four other keys out of tobacco cans," Moreland said.

"Where did you use these keys?"

"I used them at Moose Creek, Deep Creek, Meadow Creek, and Bear Creek. I didn't go into Bear Creek, as it was occupied, and I was also at Three Forks."

Again, all of the places Moreland mentioned were along or near the Selway River.

"There were snowshoe tracks at many of these places," Moreland continued. That made David Kyle think Moreland was in the Selway in the winter of either 1935-36 or 1936-37. In both those winters, game biologists made animal counts, and an unusually large number of people were in the woods.

"Where did you go from the Selway?" Mayer asked.

"I moved into the Lochsa drainage at Powell Ranger Station, where I entered and stayed a few days. From Powell I went to The Cedars on the North Fork via Horseshoe Lake and Barnard Cabin. I stayed at The Cedars about eight days."

The trip Moreland described put him on the North Fork of the Clearwater for the first time. To reach Horseshoe Lake from Powell, he had climbed a rugged divide, then descended its heavily forested northern side, traveling 63 miles in all. The names of the streams and mountains along the way, such as Shin Tangle Creek and Never Again Ridge, attested to the country's roughness.

Lewis and Clark almost starved on the same high ridges on their historic trek to the Pacific in 1805. While they were on the divide, hunger and illness so weakened Lewis that he had to be carried, and the party's travail was memorialized in such names as Hungery Creek, Horsesteak Meadow, Portable Soup Camp, Full Stomach Camp, and Colt Killed Creek. Seventy-two years later, the U.S. Cavalry left such landmarks as Pack Saddle Camp as it chased the Nez Perce over the same route in the Nez Perce War of 1877.

In 1935 the Forest Service completed a road that approximated much of Moreland's route. The winding, single-lane road, called the Lolo Motorway, was rough and difficult to travel and destined to stay that way.

Moreland crossed the road as he hiked to Horseshoe Lake Lookout. When he reached the lookout, he had a superb view of the mountains where he was to make his new home. From the base of the lookout, much of the length of Cayuse Creek, a major tributary to Kelly Creek, was visible.

Barnard Cabin, the point where Moreland emerged after cutting through the mountains, sat on the banks of Kelly Creek, which pours into the North Fork several miles downstream. A few years after Moreland passed by the cabin, an avalanche picked it up and deposited it across Kelly Creek.

Moreland forded Kelly Creek, avoiding the fate of a number of men, including Forest Service crewman Melvin Dial, who drowned while trying to cross the stream. After crossing Kelly Creek, he hiked to the stream's junction with the North Fork. He had reached his new stomping grounds.

Moreland hiked up the river to The Cedars Ranger Station, where he holed up for eight days. Then he moved around the mountains near the ranger station, which perplexed the rangers. The Cedars was an especially remote station, 62 miles from Pierce and 45 miles from Superior, Montana. It was never manned in winter, and Moreland didn't have to worry about being disturbed. He apparently thought that he had to keep moving.

Cramer, the Forest Service law enforcement officer, took over the questioning as the interview continued. "Forest Service personnel reported that someone stole items from a tent camp on Isabella Creek in the Canyon district three years ago," Cramer said. "Do you know anything about that?"

"In the spring of '42, I entered a tent camp at Isabella Creek and took some food, a pair of overalls, and a shirt," Moreland replied. "There was $3.10 and a draft registration card for W.C. Turner in the overalls. I later found some ink eradicator at either Roundtop or the Canyon and tried to change the name on the card so I could use it, but I ruined it. I figured I could use the card if I could get to the outside again."

Until he read the back of the card, he didn't know he was supposed to carry one, Moreland explained.

"Which way were you headed when you went into the camp on Isabella Creek and what time of day was it?" Cramer asked.

"I came down from Goat Ridge and entered the camp about 8:30 a.m."

After the robbery, Moreland headed up a ridge toward Black Mountain, which lay to the east, then turned west and hiked to the headwaters of Isabella Creek. From there, he turned east again and followed the St. Joe-Clearwater Divide to The Nub. His escape route covered 20 miles. It wasn't an especially long trek for him, but it was circuitous. Evidently, he relied on changing direction, as well as stealth, endurance, and woodcraft, to elude pursuers.

"Where did you go from The Nub?" Cramer asked.

"I went to the Collins Creek Cabin," Moreland answered. "This was about six days after I robbed the camp."

"How long did you stay at Collins Creek?"

"Almost a month."

"What did you take with you when you left?"

"I took a 10-pound sack of flour, some coffee, and some grease."

Moreland denied that he had stolen Bill Faucheaux's raincoat, Mackinaw, and .32-caliber pistol from the Goat Ridge Lookout.

"There was a second break-in at Goat Ridge that fall," Cramer continued. "Some food and a flashlight head-set were taken. Did you take them?"

"I took a flashlight from Goat Ridge in the fall of '42; I also took coffee and cereals."

"Some things were taken from Smith Point about a month after Goat Ridge was hit the second time. We lost some food, a kapok sleeping bag, and a flashlight. Did you take those items?"

"I have been in Smith Ridge several times, but never took a sleeping bag from there. I have taken flashlights from several places on the forest. I hid a flashlight last fall at Goat Ridge."

Cramer held his breath when he asked the next question. The field glasses Lewis had sent him were one of the few pieces of physical evidence the government had against Moreland, and Cramer hoped Moreland would admit taking them.

"A pair of field glasses and two Forest Service compasses were taken from Roundtop in the spring of 1943," he began. "They were found at Collins Creek Cabin that fall. Did you take those items?"

"I took a pair of field glasses from Roundtop, but never had a Forest Service compass of any kind."

Cramer scribbled down Moreland's admission that he took the field glasses, secretly delighted to have it.

"Where did you spend the winter of '42-43?" he asked.

"I believe I was on Snow Peak, Freezeout Mountain, and Pinchot Mountain that winter and also built a small cabin on Rutledge Creek. I got most of my food from Roundtop."

Meneely let out a low whistle. The mountains Moreland spoke of were in a rugged 25-mile swath of the St. Joe forest; Snow Peak and Freezeout Mountain were aptly named. Mayer picked up the questioning.

"When Ranger Lewis opened the Canyon station in the spring of 1943, a shutter had been pulled off a window and a pane was broken out," Mayer said. "Did you remove the shutter and break the pane?"

"I came back to the Canyon in the spring of '43, but did not break a window as I had a key and went in the door. About the only food I took was some K rations."

"Some food was taken from The Nub that spring and food and a sleeping bag were taken from Skull Creek. Did you visit those places?"

"I was up to The Nub in the spring of '43. From The Nub I went down to the Skull Creek bridge. The bridge was out and a crew was working on it. I went back up Skull Creek to a foot log and crossed, then came down to Skull Creek Cabin. I took some food but did not take a sleeping bag."

Lewis recalled that a district crewman had lived in a tent camp near Skull Creek while working on the bridge. He also remembered that a prospector named Frank Marquette had been robbed at about the same time.

"Did you break into Frank Marquette's cabin after you were at Canyon in the spring of '43?" Lewis asked.

"I went down to Marquette's cabin, but did not break in," Moreland replied. "All I had to do was turn the lock. It wasn't fastened. I also built a fire in the woodshed with some bark."

"Where else did you go during the 1943 season?" Cramer asked Moreland.

"I went to Cold Springs in the fall during hunting season. There were hunters camped at Mush Camp and Moscow Bar, so I went over the ridge to Monumental Buttes and then on to Bear Skull, where I killed a deer."

Moreland had crossed the St. Joe-Clearwater Divide, making a trip of 52 miles after seeing the hunters. The rangers wondered if contact with others frightened him or if he constantly feared that he was being pursued.

The binoculars from Roundtop had turned up at the Collins Creek Cabin about the same time that Moreland saw the hunters, but Moreland could not have brought them over the divide on the trip he just described. He was headed in the wrong direction; he must have made another trip over the divide.

He had obtained his rifle from the Skull Creek Cabin a month earlier, and food was taken from Roundtop a few days later. On that trip, he was again headed in the wrong direction to bring the binoculars over the divide. He must have crossed the divide a third time in a little more than a month.

"Rations were taken from Roundtop in the fall of '43," Cramer said. "Did you take them?"

"I took some Army rations from Roundtop and some tea, then went down the Twin Creeks trail about two miles and made camp," Moreland replied.

Cramer knew of a second burglary at Roundtop that fall, and he asked

Moreland how many times he had been in the station that autumn.

"I was in Roundtop about four times that fall, and men were in there two of those times," Moreland answered. "I have also been at Elk Prairie three or four times and used keys to go in."

Mayer asked Moreland how long he had been in the Flat Creek Cabin when Clyde Cole and Louis Holt surprised him in March of 1944.

"I had only been in the cabin about 40 minutes when the two men caught me," Moreland replied.

"Where did you go?"

"I went downriver almost to Skull Creek that night and on to Skull Creek the next morning for breakfast. Then I went to Canyon, then down to Hughes' cabin, where I crossed the river and went on to Camp T. At Camp T I found some grub, but a bear had been in the building and torn up the place. I found some peanut butter, which I took, and went down the flume, across the river and up to Boehls Cabin, then on toward Elk River."

Moreland had traveled more than 40 miles, crossing the river twice and changing direction several times after Holt and Cole interrupted his dinner. The Forest Service had not heard from him again until Roark and Horner cut his trail, and the rangers wanted to know where he had been in the intervening time.

"Where did you spend last summer?" Lewis asked.

"I stayed most of the summer along the Camp T flume," Moreland said. "I had a camp on the hillside near the flume."

Moreland had spent the winter near Gold Creek, which was 30 miles west of Canyon and off national forest land.

"I made a lean-to out of some boards about a mile up from the mouth of Gold Creek," he explained. "I lived on venison and cereals from Camp T; I believe there are blankets, shoes, and trousers at this camp yet."

"Did you make any trips last fall?" Lewis asked.

"I made a couple of trips down the river for some distance, but I heard people so I went up on the hill. I made two rafts and left one on each side of the river so no one would know which way I had gone."

Moreland's desire to avoid others struck his interviewers as obsessive.

"Did you do anything to throw people off your trail while you were in the woods?" Meneely asked.

"At one time I had an extra pair of shoes on sticks, and I made tracks going in the opposite direction so no one could tell which way I had traveled."

"You made footprints with an extra pair of shoes?" Meneely asked. "How?"

"Like this." Moreland stood and walked in a slouch across the room, moving his clenched fists up and down as if stamping images on the floor. "I thought that might throw the dear rangers off my trail," he added.

"Do you have references of any kind, anyone who could vouch for you or provide information about you?" Mayer asked.

"I do not know anyone who has personal knowledge of me or can give any information about me."

"Why did you go into the woods in the first place?"

"I got in trouble over a girl on the sheep ranch near Mountain Home. The girl's name was Rose."

"What do you mean you got in trouble over her?"

"I believe the girl's mother was going to frame me. The mother was cooking on the sheep ranch and was quite intimate with a man who was there."

"How was the girl's mother going to frame you?"

"She thought I had some money and she knew that I had been in prison, so she was going to tell the law that I was in trouble with her daughter and get what money I had. I had about $100 coming from the sheepman, and I gave the girl about $50 so she could go to school."

"How old was the girl?"

"She was about 16. She wrote three letters to me after she went to school. They came from either Kirkland or Arnwood in Washington. She said she had been boat riding on Lake Washington."

"I see," Mayer replied. He had no idea whether to believe the story.

"Here," Mayer said, handing Moreland a photograph of Frank Davis, whom Roark had arrested when he first tried to track down Moreland. "Have you seen this man?" Mayer asked.

"I believe so, but I don't know where. I may have seen him at Skull Creek Cabin, Canyon Ranger Station, or Smith Cabin."

"When?"

"Within the last two years."

Mayer nodded and then paused. The interview had gone on for a long time, and he had the answers he needed.

"That is all I have," he said, turning to Cramer. "Do you have anything further?"

"Just one more question," Cramer replied, turning to Moreland, "The field glasses found at Collins Creek Cabin were taken from Roundtop, right?"

"You already asked me that," Moreland snapped.

"I'm just trying to keep things straight."

"All right, I'll tell you another damn time. I took a flashlight and field glasses at Roundtop and later left them at Collins cabin."

The six men waited while a stenographer typed a statement detailing Moreland's confession. Then, as Mayer, Cramer, Kyle, Lewis, and Meneely watched, Moreland signed the statement.

The statement was a damning piece of evidence. It said, "During the time I was in the mountains, I entered almost every Forest Service lookout and cabin in the North Fork of the Clearwater area and also entered cabins in the Salmon River area, the St. Joe River area, and in the Sawtooth Mountain area. I used a key I had made to make all of these entries. I knew it was unlawful because I saw Forest Service signs which said it was unlawful to break or enter. I usually took food from these places, but also took other supplies such as flashlights, blankets, sleeping bags, and sometimes clothing that happened to be there. I once took a portable radio...I think it must have been about the time Roosevelt was running for president the first time that I went into the mountains."

Mayer filed a criminal complaint charging Moreland with failure to carry a Selective Service card and failure to register for the draft. The charges would give the authorities something to hold Moreland on while they investigated the break-ins. Moreland was arraigned that night before U.S. Commissioner E.B. Steele. He waived his right to a preliminary hearing and tried to plead guilty in the arraignment, but Steele rejected his plea. The law required that he enter his plea before a U.S. district judge, and Steele was not a judge. Steele set bail at $600.

Moreland could not meet bail, and the next day he was taken to the Nez Perce County Jail in Lewiston, which had been approved for incarceration of federal prisoners.

He also had a doctor's examination. The rangers were surprised to learn that the man who could make 70-mile hikes in the mountains was suffering from malnutrition.

EIGHT

The charges against Moreland didn't stick. At the time he went into the woods, he was not required to register for the draft, and U.S. District Attorney John Carver thought he couldn't prove Moreland had learned of the requirement. Despite Moreland's signed statement, Carver also thought the evidence was insufficient to convict Moreland for entering government buildings. He instructed Mayer to drop the charges against Moreland.

Cramer made a vain attempt to persuade Carver to prosecute Moreland. In a report enumerating Moreland's break-ins, Cramer complained, "This is only a small percentage of the total depredations committed by Moreland against government property."

Cramer added that it was suspected Moreland had fled to the mountains after committing a serious crime. He pointed out that a sleeping bag and hand ax Moreland was carrying when he was caught carried the Forest Service brand. Still, Carver refused to prosecute.

A week after Moreland's arrest, U.S. Army Air Force Lt. Bud Ripley, who was in England, came across an account of Moreland's apprehension in "The Stars and Stripes," the serviceman's newspaper. Other serviceman's papers also carried stories about the arrest; one, the "New

Guinea News," reported the capture of the "human coyote."

Moreland was moved from the jail at Lewiston back to the jail at Orofino to await action on state charges. While he sat in his cell, the FBI investigated whether he was involved in the Mattson kidnapping in Tacoma in 1937, but he was cleared of that crime, which remained unsolved. Moreland still faced state burglary charges. Local officials, however, were content to let him sit; they were unsure what else to do with him.

At least part of Moreland's story checked out. He had told the rangers that a man almost ran him down after he stole a rifle at Lantz's Bar on the Salmon River. Frank Lantz, the sole resident of Lantz's Bar, confirmed he had chased a thief who stole a rifle from his cabin. The thief dropped the weapon just before Lantz caught up with him.

A Johnson Flying Service pilot recalled that someone had attempted to start a plane at the Chamberlain Basin airfield during the summer that Moreland visited the basin. The pilot said the intruder failed to get the plane started, which jibed with Moreland's story.

Through a check of the FBI's fingerprint files, Mayer confirmed that Moreland was sentenced on May 8, 1921, to one to three years in the state prison at Florence, Arizona. The charge was burglary; he was sentenced under the name John Howard. The fingerprint files also confirmed that Moreland was imprisoned on Oct. 23, 1922, at the state penitentiary at Little Rock, Arkansas. In that case, he was sentenced under the name John Williams to two to four years on a grand larceny charge.

Moreland was still in jail in Orofino when Moton Roark came to visit him in March. Roark carried a sack of oranges and a pint of ice cream as he tiptoed down the jail hallway. He had surprised the wily Moreland once before, and he wanted to see if he could do it again. Moreland was sitting on his bunk, seemingly lost in thought as Roark neared his cell. He did not look in Roark's direction, but suddenly piped up.

"Hello, you wolf," he said.

Both men laughed; a deputy let Roark into Moreland's cell.

"How are they treating you?" Roark asked.

"Better than those rangers treated me on the way out from Canyon."

"What happened?"

"They ran my legs off in those snowshoes. I kept up with Lewis, but I couldn't keep up with that big Indian. My legs got cramped up and I fell."

"Bill, Louis Holt was just doing what he was told to do. He's a good man."

"Maybe so," Moreland said. "By the way, look at my pictures."

Moreland had pasted a magazine photograph of Shirley Temple to the cell wall and had drawn a crude picture of an airplane on the wall beside the photograph.

"Bill, didn't you ever want to come out of the woods in all that time?" Roark asked.

"I started out once, near New Meadows," Moreland replied. "An airplane flew over dropping something. Branches were breaking out of trees; I thought the men in that plane were trying to kill me, so I ran back into the woods.

"Later, I found salt blocks on the ground. They were dropping salt for the elk, and I thought they were trying to kill me." He smiled and shook his head.

"Were you scared at other times?" Roark asked.

"Once. I woke up in the night and heard a thumping noise. I couldn't tell what it was. I figured out later it was a cottontail rabbit, hitting its foot on the ground."

Moreland told Roark he had injured himself seriously just once during his years in the woods. He fell as he was chopping footholds in a sheet of ice that covered a steep hillside. He slid about 150 feet down the hill, injuring his side so badly he couldn't move. He laid there until the next day, when he dragged himself to a nearby cave. He stayed in the cave for days until he felt like traveling again, but his side hurt for months afterwards.

"Here, I brought you one more thing, even though I don't use the stuff myself," Roark said. He gave the Ridgerunner a sack of Bull Durham cigarette tobacco and a package of cigarette papers.

"Why don't you stay for dinner?" Moreland asked. He scrambled a panful of eggs in the jail kitchen for himself and Roark.

On Oct. 4, 1945, eight months after he was captured, Moreland pleaded guilty in state district court to a burglary charge. He was given a five-year suspended sentence and was released.

The authorities had found a job for him herding sheep near Asotin, Washington, but within days Moreland was back on the North Fork of the Clearwater.

Perd Hughes, a year-round resident of the river, was the first to learn that the Ridgerunner had returned to his old haunts. Hughes arrived at his lodge after an afternoon's fishing to find that a rifle and a pair of snowshoes had been stolen. He thought he had seen the last of his rifle and footgear, but the next night he heard a knock at the door. When he opened the door, Moreland held the rifle out to him butt first.

"I brought your things back," Moreland said. "I didn't want to be out there with you chasing me."

"You're the Ridgerunner, aren't you?" Hughes asked.

"Yes."

Hughes looked over the little man's shoulder; heavy wet snowflakes fell at a sharp angle onto the river.

"Come in," Hughes said. "I've heard about your troubles."

Moreland's clothes were sopping wet. He walked straight to Hughes' woodstove and held out his hands to warm them. The light from Hughes' lantern lit his whiskered face and black eyes.

"Would you like a drink of whiskey?" Hughes offered. "It will warm you up."

"I'll have a small one," Moreland said.

Hughes poured a few sips of whiskey into a tin cup and handed it to Moreland. He poured himself a larger drink and settled into a chair near the stove.

"Sit down," he said.

Moreland ignored a chair next to Hughes' chair and turned a block of firewood on end so he could sit on it.

"This is a nice place," Moreland said. "Have you been here long?"

"I came here in 1929, right after Black Tuesday, the day the stock market crashed," Hughes replied. "I had just gotten a college teaching certificate, but I didn't think there would be many openings for teachers after the market crashed. I've been here ever since."

"It's a good place, this river."

"Yes, it is. I lease my place from the state. When I first came, it cost me about a thousand dollars to buy my supplies and get set up here. I paid that off the first year."

Hughes took a sip of whiskey. It was hot in his throat.

"Where are you from?" he asked.

"I'm from the East," Moreland answered. "I grew up in reform schools."

Moreland set his cup on the floor and looked back over his shoulder into the dark corners of the big cabin. It was an impressive place.

"More whiskey?" Hughes asked.

"No."

"I'll tell you what," Hughes said. "Why don't you stay here with me this winter? I've got plenty of room and you're down on your luck. We can do a little hunting, and you can help me run my trap lines. What do you say?"

"I'll stay," Moreland said, "but I'm leaving come spring."

"Fair enough."

Hughes' cabin had many of the comforts of home. The lodge-size building was big enough to sleep 21 people. In the spring, PFI's river-drive crews slept there, and the company paid Hughes for the accommodations.

The clever Hughes was an expert gardener who grew his own tobacco. He also kept horses and chickens and had dug a root cellar into the side of the mountain. The cellar kept vegetables and meats cool even on the hottest days of summer.

Hughes also had built a round wooden tank beside the building and diverted water into it from a spring. He stocked the tank with trout. Guests were expected to dip in with a net that stood next to the tank and select the fish they wanted for breakfast. Hughes, an excellent cook, then killed and prepared the fish, surely some of the freshest trout ever served.

Hughes had supervised the building of the log flume at PFI's Camp X, which was near his lodge on the north side of the river west of Canyon. He also surveyed a logging road that PFI built up a mountain behind his lodge. The mountain, known as Hughes Point, was named after him.

In the winter, the road to Hughes' place was plowed as far as Camp X, which was seven miles west. Hughes plowed the road on to his cabin until the snow got higher than the headlights on his vehicles. Then he parked his vehicles and walked the rest of the winter.

The wiry, five-foot-10, 160-pound woodsman thought nothing of strapping on his snowshoes and hiking to Elk River, which was 23 miles from his cabin. He snowshoed so much that the muscles on his shins were unusually well developed; he stayed in such good condition that he could do handstands when he was in his 60s.

Hughes had many visitors, and Moreland was usually quiet when they came to the lodge. He would never confirm that he had made an unexplained footprint or noise.

One man, Holbert Miller, was certain he had spoken to Moreland on the trail before Moreland was captured. Miller also believed he had followed one of Moreland's false trails, and he asked Moreland about that one night.

"I was coming down the hill to Perd's cabin when I saw a set of snowshoe tracks," Miller explained. "I followed the tracks for a couple of miles and found another set of tracks headed in the same direction. I continued on, but the second set of tracks stopped just as suddenly as it started. I never could figure that out, but I'll bet that was you, Bill, putting your snowshoes on backwards and going back the way you had come."

"Oh no, that wasn't me," Moreland insisted. "I never did that."

Miller remained convinced that Moreland had left the trail. He also believed that the little man had been inside a friend's cabin when he checked on the cabin while his friend was away.

Miller remembered that smoke was coming from the chimney when he rode up to the building. He did not go to the door, however. He wanted to alert whoever was inside to his presence, so he walked his horse to the barn, saying in a loud voice, "I'm going to rub down my horse, and then I'll be up to the cabin." When he returned, the cabin was empty. Miller suspected that the Ridgerunner had been inside. He had the feeling that the man was running from nothing.

During the winter that Moreland spent with Hughes, Moreland occasionally accompanied Hughes to Elk River, where the two were overnight guests at Miller's home. Moreland didn't buy much when he was in town. He browsed around the drugstore or had a beer at the bar, but he never drank more than one beer at a time, and he seldom stayed in town longer than a day or two. Miller thought that Moreland came to town solely to break the routine of life in the woods. He didn't seem to need the company of others and he bought little in the way of supplies.

Hughes and Moreland got along well. One night the two men visited Camp X, which Hughes watched for Potlatch when logging operations were shut down. It was early spring, and a big bear, gaunt from hibernation, tried to get into the bunkhouse where the two men were staying.

The bear stood on its hind legs and pawed at the sill of a window, which was five feet off the ground. Hughes and Moreland yelled at the animal, but it continued to slap at the window. Finally, Moreland fired a shot through the window. Since he was at point-blank range, he had to have hit the bear. The animal ran off. Hughes thought Moreland had shot the bear unnecessarily.

Moreland's thorough knowledge of the forest impressed Hughes. The two men were atop a mountain far from Hughes' cabin late one afternoon when dense fog set in. Hughes had not been in the area before, and his unfamiliarity with the terrain made him uneasy. The two men picked their way over rocks and fallen logs, but darkness neared while they were still miles from the cabin. Hughes wanted to stop for the night, but Moreland insisted that he knew the way. Hughes reluctantly followed Moreland through the darkness. They could hardly see where they were going, but they reached Hughes' cabin without once having to double back. Hughes knew he could not have made the trip alone.

Moreland made good on his promise to leave when spring came; it was apparent that he wanted to be on his own. During the next few years he worked for PFI three times and for the Clearwater Timber Protective Assocation and the Potlatch Timber Protective Association on three occasions.

The timber-protective associations, operating with funds from assessments on the thousands of acres of timberland in the St. Joe-Clearwater area, manned fire-fighting camps in the woods. The Potlatch Timber Protective Association, or PTPA, had a camp near the confluence of the Little North Fork and the North Fork of the Clearwater, which was right where Moreland wanted to be. The camp, named after an early day settler, was called Boehl's Cabin.

Boehl's Cabin sat in a wide flat of cedars; its bunkhouses accommodated 21 men who worked at a variety of fire-prevention jobs, finishing up the season in November by burning branches and tree tops left over from logging. Dwain Space, who ran the camp, interviewed Moreland when he applied for work.

"What can you do?" Space, a hefty woodsman, asked Moreland.

"I can handle powder. I worked in blasting for the CTPA," Moreland replied, referring to the Clearwater Timber Protective Association.

"Can you fight fire? That's what we do here is fight fire."

"Sure," Moreland said. "I can walk to a fire anywhere."

"I'll bet you can, too," Space said.

While he talked to Moreland, Space's mind was at work. The woods camp bosses of the North Fork area had agreed to keep Moreland working if they could. They thought it was better to have him on the job than running around the woods stealing things. Apparently, it was Space's turn to employ Moreland.

"I'm going to put you on as a smokechaser, but that won't be full time," Space said. "When there aren't any fires, you'll be pimpin' for the Cat."

By "pimpin' for the Cat," Space meant that Moreland would be helping a bulldozer operator.

"Some of the men who work in this camp have had things disappear over the years," Space continued. "They might think you took their belongings, but I think they'll give you a chance. I don't want to have things turning up missing, though."

"You won't."

Like many others who worked in the woods, Space was fascinated by Moreland's 13-year odyssey in the forest.

"How did you keep from freezing to death when you stayed out all those years?" Space asked.

"I slept sitting up by the fire," Moreland said. "When the fire burned down, I'd get cold and wake up and put more wood on."

"Why did you let those rangers catch you?"

"They never would have caught me if I hadn't had a toothache. My tooth hurt so bad I was looking down instead of paying attention to what was going on around me."

"That was pretty remarkable, the way you lived in the mountains all those years," Space said. "Did you have any trouble with bears getting into your food?"

"The dear things got into my caches once in a while," Moreland replied. "I scared the daylights out of one of them. He was coming down the trail, and I saw him before he saw me. I got up on a stump and jumped at him when he came close. He took off running. The next day I walked 30 miles up the river. I saw some people who told me that contemptible bear was still running when he came by."

Space laughed at the improbable story; even though Moreland was an odd duck, he might work out all right.

Moreland worked tirelessly. He set "chokers"—loops in the ends of cables—around logs so a bulldozer could pull the logs out of the woods. He lugged blasting powder for crewmen who "shot stumps" to blow them out of the ground. Space wanted an exact accounting of the explosives when Moreland was around.

Moreland got along well with Space, who thought it was curious that Moreland would take his camera to town and snap pictures of buildings when most people shot photographs in the forest. Moreland explained that he saw a lot of the woods, but didn't see much of town.

Moreland liked to talk about the sights he had seen in the mountains. When Space planned to travel to an unfamiliar place, he would ask Moreland to tell him about the spot. Moreland's descriptions proved to be uncannily accurate. After finding one place to be exactly as Moreland described it, Space told some of the men, "He's been everywhere in this forest; he's seen every square inch of it."

When the fire season ended and the PTPA laid off its crew, Moreland lived in the brush as he had before his capture. After running into him unexpectedly in the woods one spring, Space's wife, Ada, recruited him to return to work. She was off the trail picking berries near Boehl's Cabin when Moreland came along. Moreland didn't see her as he approached. When he came up, she said, "Hello, Shorty." Moreland jumped in surprise.

"Dwain has been expecting you to come to work," she said. "Why don't you go up to camp? He's got a job for you."

Moreland was a sight. His clothes were tattered and torn, and his whiskers were long. He carried a string of trout with him.

"Can the cook fry these trout for supper?" he asked.

"Yes."

"Then I'll go to work."

Moreland dropped off his fish at the cookhouse, then went to the bathhouse. He showered, shaved, and put on clothes he had left in camp the fall before. He ate his fish for supper and went to work the next morning.

Moreland relished telling yarns to his fellow crew members, and he told them well. He launched into the stories during the evening meal, talking just loud enough so his audience could hear. He looked down at his plate while he spoke, and all conversation stopped when he started a tale.

"I saw a fence right out in the middle of a farmer's field when I was in Arkansas," he began one night. "It was a white picket fence, a little one, built in a square. There wasn't anything inside that I could see, but people kept walking up, looking over and laughing.

"I went over to look. There were footprints inside the fence. A fellow told me those were the footprints of the first man in Arkansas who wore shoes."

It was obvious, however, that Moreland wasn't totally at peace with his new existence. Even though he had a small appetite, he packed a large lunch; some of the men suspected he stashed the extra food for winter.

Moreland didn't come to the cookhouse for dinner when officials from other agencies visited Boehl's Cabin, which happened often because of the camp's central location. Odd signs were nailed to trees near camp, and Moreland was suspected of putting them up. One of the signs read, "What gave Dwain Space the right to teach the kids at Boehl's Cabin how to dynamite fish in the river?"

Space knew the signs were preposterous and thought that no one would take them seriously. He laughed at them and did nothing.

Some of the crewmen teased Moreland. He accepted the joshing when he was in good spirits, but not when he was moody; he became furious when he was teased about women.

He was unusually quiet in the cookhouse one night. Some of the men urged him to tell a story, but Moreland refused.

Finally, one of the men went too far. "I guess 'Shorty' has run out of lies," he said. Moreland leaped to his feet and stormed out. He returned a few minutes later with a .22-caliber revolver strapped to his hip. The meal was completed in silence.

A few nights later, Moreland left camp in the darkness and did not return. Space suspected that he had been beaten up. The same thing had happened when he worked for the CTPA, ending his employment there.

PFI, Moreland's next employer, was far bigger than the timber-protective associations. The company, the biggest timber firm in north-central Idaho, began accumulating its immense holdings in 1900, when Frederick Weyerhaeuser and fellow executive John A. Humbird bought Northern Pacific Railroad Co. scrip giving them rights to 40,000 acres of land in the Clearwater country. Their holdings became the nucleus of the Clearwater Timber Co., which in 1927 owned 236,125 acres of timber land.

The Weyerhaeusers also formed the Potlatch Timber Co. to the north in 1906 and a third firm known as the Rutledge Timber Co. The three firms merged in 1931; at the time, the Clearwater Timber Co. operated a huge new sawmill at Lewiston. After the merger, PFI built an even bigger pulp and paper mill there.

Moreland worked in the company's woods and river camps. The woods camps, such as Camp 14, had numerical designations. Timber cut there was hauled on the company's rail lines. Letter names, such as Camp T, were given to the river camps, where timber was cut for an annual spring log drive down the swollen North Fork of the Clearwater.

The camps were rustic places consisting of movable wooden buildings set on heavy timbers. The men who lived in the camps worked hard and played hard. One winter four men imprisoned at different penitentiaries wrote Fred Hansen, the boss at Camp T, to request income tax withholding statements. All four had worked at Camp T the previous summer.

Many of the loggers drank and gambled when they went to town. Into the 1950s Pierce, which had just 910 people, served the loggers with two brothels and 13 bars. The owner of one of the brothels cleaned out her safe one night when a fire broke out. She admonished her clients to "take care of my chinchillas, boys. I've got what I want right here."

When the loggers were in camp, they tended to business. Drinking was not allowed, and since the loggers burned prodigious amounts of energy, eating was a serious matter. Absolute silence was observed during meals. When a logger spoke, it was only to utter such words as "blood" when he wanted the ketchup or "punk" to ask for the bread. Hotcakes were "liver pads," prunes were "Potlatch strawberries," and cheese was "roughlock." The loggers expected, and got, the finest in steaks, roasts, and hams. The cooks baked homemade pies and bread daily.

Moreland entered the world of the logging camps at Bovill, where he greased Cats on the night shift. Bovill, the site of PFI's Camp 42, was west of the St. Joe-Clearwater Divide.

A major focus of PFI's operations in the area was the decking of logs along the Little North Fork. Buford O'Keefe, one of Moreland's fellow workers, built log decks along the river from July until the annual log drive the following spring. The parallel 16-foot-wide, 50-foot-high twin decks stretched for a mile and a half. The saws at PFI's big mill at Lewiston cut 30 million board feet of lumber every year from the logs.

Moreland told O'Keefe about a cave where he holed up not far from the decking area. The cave, which was three miles up the Little North Fork from Boehl's Cabin, was well above the trail on the side of a cliff. It went into the hillside about 20 feet and had a ceiling that was about 20 feet high.

The cave was dry, and Moreland hauled his water up in a bucket using a rope. He said he once spent a winter in the cave, though he almost froze to death. Empty food cans and the ashes of his fires littered the interior. When Potlatch began logging nearby, Moreland put up signs on the road near Perd Hughes' place that read, "Gateway to Hell."

O'Keefe found Moreland to be a pleasant man who preferred to be left alone, but he had a run-in with Moreland at a tavern in Bovill. O'Keefe thought Moreland was using unacceptable language in front of several women, including his wife. He told Moreland to clean up his language. He claimed that Moreland pulled a knife.

O'Keefe picked up a chair, and Moreland left the tavern. Moreland had not tried to use the knife; he acted later as if nothing had happened.

As was his custom, Moreland left his job at Bovill after he had made a few hundred dollars. He needed little money, and he generally didn't hold a job long. He later hired on as a cat greaser at Camp 60 on the Clearwater side of the St. Joe-Clearwater Divide. His successful stint there convinced Howard Bradbury, PFI's logging superintendent at Headquarters, to hire him in the spring of 1948. Bradbury called Fred Hansen into his office to discuss putting Moreland to work.

"I want you to put the Ridgerunner on out at Camp T," Bradbury said.

"There was trouble when he worked for the 'association,' " Hansen warned. "He was involved in a fight in the bunkhouse."

"I know, but I would rather have him on one of our crews than running around out in the woods some place. They say he's quiet most of the time. He might be better off if he could work alone. Put him down on the river. He can work there and live by himself. You handle the men well, and I want him working for you."

"All right," Hansen agreed.

Hansen put Moreland on as a flume walker. It seemed like an ideal job. Moreland would live alone in a cabin at the mouth of Elkberry Creek two miles from Camp T.

PFI's flumes were big wooden troughs standing head high and running for miles through the forest. Water from streams was diverted into the v-shaped flumes to carry logs to the river. The logs moved at high speed, plunging out the end of the flumes and falling into deep holes in the river with a booming splash. The logs were retrieved and stacked in huge decks until spring runoff swelled the North Fork and they could be floated to Lewiston.

The flumes were an integral part of PFI's operations. The company sawed 170 million board feet of lumber—enough to build 15,000 homes—from the logs carried by just one of the flumes between 1930 and 1942.

Moreland's job was to walk up the Camp T flume each morning while another flume walker came down from camp. The two men made sure the flume was in good repair and clear of debris. If a plank were missing from the side or a pile of debris had formed, the heavy logs could bash through the side of the flume. Other logs would follow, usually falling to the forest floor in a steep or wooded place where they were impossible to retrieve. Valuable timber was lost when such a mishap occurred, and the flume could be shut down for hours.

When the flume walkers met each morning, they called Camp T on one of the telephones mounted on the side of the flume. If they had found no problems, they said, "Everything is clear," and the day's quota of logs began moving down the big wooden trough.

Things went well during Moreland's first summer on the Camp T crew. Hansen felt sorry for the little man and invited him home to dinner when he was in camp. Moreland babysat Hansen's children when the camp boss and his wife were gone. Hansen couldn't get Moreland to bathe regularly, but since Moreland usually worked by himself, that wasn't much of a problem.

Moreland seemed to enjoy his job and to be grateful for it. It allowed him to pursue the lifestyle he preferred. Bradbury hoped the answer to a problem had been found.

When logging operations ended for the season, Moreland asked for permission to spend the winter in the company cabin at the end of the flume. Bradbury agreed.

*N*INE

One afternoon during the winter Fred Hansen hiked to the river from Camp T to check on Moreland. When Hansen arrived at the mouth of Elkberry Creek, a little dog was outside the door of Moreland's shack. The dog, a mutt, yapped as Hansen walked up. A voice inside said, "Stay out, you son-of-a-bitch."

Hansen walked around to the side of the clapboard building and peered through the window. Moreland sat on the edge of his bunk inside, staring into space, working his jaws back and forth, gritting his teeth audibly.

Hansen knew that Moreland had directed his epithet at the dog, and he smiled. Moreland didn't know he had a visitor.

Hansen went around to the door and knocked. Moreland opened the door and exclaimed, "Jesus, Jesus jumped-up Jesus, am I glad to see somebody."

"Hello, Bill," Hansen said. "I brought you some steaks and pork chops. I brought you some magazines, too."

Moreland took a copy of "U.S. News & World Report" from the stack of magazines Hansen had brought. He eagerly flicked through the pages as he sat down on his bunk. Hansen came in, closed the door behind him and sat in the only chair in the little building.

Moreland held up the opened magazine and showed Hansen a photograph of Margaret Truman, President Harry S Truman's daughter.

"Who do you suppose old Harry is saving her for?" he asked. "Do you suppose he's saving her for me?"

Both men laughed at Moreland's preposterous notion.

"How is the winter going, Bill?" Hansen asked.

"It's going fine," Moreland replied, "but I had a scare a while back."

"What happened?"

"Two big fellows came to the door. I was afraid they were after me at first, but they said, "We wanted to thank you for all the hotcakes you floated to us down on the Columbia last winter.'"

Moreland and Hansen laughed again. The Columbia was more than a hundred miles from the North Fork of the Clearwater; no hotcake could float that far.

"I've got my money hidden in this cabin, Fred," Moreland declared. "I'll bet you can't find it."

"Bill, I don't want to look for your money," Hansen replied.

"Go ahead. You won't be able to find it."

"I have no idea where it is. Is it near me?"

"It's right here."

Moreland jumped to his feet and grabbed the pepper shaker off the table. He unscrewed the cap, emptied the pepper onto the table, and picked a compact ball of rubber bands from the pepper. Moreland peeled the rubber bands from the ball. Within a moment, he had exposed a wad of paper. Then he pulled the wad apart. It was made up of his paychecks. He unfolded the checks and laid them flat on the table for Hansen to see.

"I've got all my paychecks here from last summer," Moreland explained. "Men have sat right where you are and put pepper on their sandwiches, but they didn't know they had my paychecks in their hand."

"That's pretty clever, Bill."

The tall camp boss rose and walked to the window. Storm clouds had formed as he walked to Moreland's shack, and snow was falling heavily.

"I'd better get going, Bill," Hansen said. "The snow is coming down pretty hard."

Hansen buttoned his coat.

"Won't you move up to the camp, Bill?" Hansen asked. "You might hurt yourself or get sick down here and nobody would know. There's a telephone at the camp, and people at the office in Headquarters can call to make sure you're all right. There's nobody around camp now so you would have the place to yourself. There's plenty of food, and you could take a bath once in a while."

"I like it down here by the river," Moreland replied. "I'm going to stay."

"Okay. Suit yourself."

Hansen strapped on his snowshoes and hiked back up the trail. He waved to Moreland, who stood in the doorway long enough to return the wave before he went inside.

Hansen looked at Moreland's shack. Blocks of cured tamarack, the best firewood in the forest, sat unused near the cabin where Hansen had instructed two crewmen to stack it. Yet Moreland was burning green branches in his stove. The green wood put out very little heat, and it was cold in the cabin, but Moreland didn't seem to notice. Perhaps after all the years he had spent in the brush, the cold no longer bothered him. Hansen shrugged his shoulders and walked on.

Despite Hansen's best efforts, things began to go sour between Moreland and PFI. In the summer of 1949, Moreland bought gifts for logging superintendent Howard Bradbury's daughter, Marjorie. He sent the girl a blanket, a string of pearls, and a ring; the gifts upset her mother.

Moreland also lavished his generosity on Bernajean Edelblute, Marjorie Bradbury's cousin and the daughter of Lawrence "Boots" Edelblute, the assistant superintendent of logging at Headquarters. Bernajean, who was 18, worked as a flunky in the kitchen at Camp T. When she came out of the cookhouse to ring the dinner bell one night, Moreland tugged gently on a lock of her blonde hair. She thought nothing of it. On another evening, Moreland was waiting for her when she left the cookhouse.

"Here, Bernajean, you take this," Moreland said, handing the girl a folded newspaper. She opened the paper and found his paycheck inside.

"You're too nice a girl to have to work as a flunky," Moreland explained. "You go home and I'll send you my paycheck every month."

The girl didn't know what to say. She handed the paycheck back to Moreland and told her father what had happened. "Boots" Edelblute was upset. He talked with Hansen about firing Moreland, but Hansen said the incident had nothing to do with Moreland's work, which was satisfactory. Hansen did, however, tell Moreland of Edelblute's feelings. "I'll shoot his damn legs out from under him," Moreland exclaimed.

"Bill, don't talk like that," Hansen admonished.

Bernajean still had no fear of Moreland, but later he left notes where he knew she would find them. It was clear that he fantasized about her. Although his intentions seemed to be platonic, he suggested falsely that she had a sexual relationship with a young crewman whom she had known in school. The notes frightened the girl, and it embarrassed her to give them to her uncle, as her father suggested. She knew, however, that she was leaving the woods soon to attend college. She was sure that would resolve the problem.

Moreland stayed on the job, but his moodiness became more frequent. He spent less time at Camp T and more time down at the river, where he could be alone. He constantly wore a gun, which made the other men nervous, and as the stories of his unusual behavior spread, several workers complained about Moreland's gun.

Hansen and the cookhouse crew opened Camp T for the 1950 work season on April 17. The next day Hansen reported to Bradbury that he had had an argument with Moreland on the phone. The Ridgerunner claimed that he had worked all winter and the company owed him for his labor. Hansen and Bradbury knew Moreland had been laid off at Christmas, when ice clogged the flume and ended operations.

On April 19, Hansen and Charles "Red" McCollister, a veteran PFI lumberjack, made a trip into the woods to talk to Moreland. They towed a load of lumber on a sled behind their bulldozer; they planned to deliver the lumber at Moreland's cabin, but the real reason for the trip was to check on Moreland.

Hansen and McCollister spotted Moreland as their bulldozer clanked up to his cabin. He was nearby, chopping ice out of the flume with an ax; he wore his .22-caliber pistol on his hip, and his rifle rested against the side of the flume.

Hansen and McCollister hailed Moreland. He walked over to the bulldozer, but did not greet the two men.

"Here's your last paycheck for the season, Bill," Hansen said, handing Moreland an envelope.

Moreland opened the envelope and removed the check. Then he tore it to bits and threw the shreds of blue paper on the snow. "That's not enough," he declared. "I've been working all winter."

"Bill, you were laid off at Christmas, and you knew you were laid off," Hansen replied. "Bradbury told me that he wrote you personally when he heard that you were still working and told you that you were laid off. He said he had the note delivered to your cabin."

"I'm not working for The Potlatch," Moreland exclaimed. "I'm working for The Weyerhaeuser out of St. Paul. I'm a special agent for The Weyerhaeuser."

"I'm Weyerhaeuser's representative here," Hansen said, assuming a proper role in that PFI and Weyerhaeuser Co. had common interests. "I say you were laid off."

Suddenly, Moreland pulled his pistol. Before he could bring the pistol up, Hansen jumped down from the bulldozer and grabbed Moreland's wrist, pinning the gun to Moreland's side. The weapon pointed at the ground.

Hansen, who was much larger than Moreland, held Moreland's wrist tight. The two men stood locked in a near motionless struggle.

McCollister, who had never seen Moreland before, was too stunned to move. He had thought he would be helping Hansen unload lumber. Now he was part of a very messy situation.

"I've never heard of a guy getting shot while unloading lumber," McCollister thought.

Hansen, his voice strained with tension, tried to calm Moreland.

"Let's put that son-of-a-bitch away, Bill," he said. "We don't need that out."

Hansen eased his grip on Moreland's arm bit by bit. He could tell that Moreland was no longer struggling to free the gun, and he did not believe that Moreland would shoot him. Finally, he took his hand away and stepped back.

Moreland put the pistol back in its holster, then stomped off toward his cabin. He went inside and slammed the door behind him.

Hansen was shaken. He looked at McCollister, who let out a low whistle. McCollister started the bulldozer. Hansen climbed aboard and the two men left without attempting to talk to Moreland again. That night Hansen telephoned Bradbury and told him what had happened.

"I went to a board of directors meeting at Lewiston today," Bradbury said. "Some board members said the company should offer Moreland a sum of money to leave the country and not come back. I told them I didn't think he would live up to his end of the bargain."

"He doesn't cash the paychecks we give him now," Hansen replied. "He isn't interested in money. Even if he accepted an offer, he would be back in a few days. He loves it down by the river, and he is going to stay."

"I'd better talk to him and see if I can get him to stop wearing that gun," Bradbury said. "Call him tomorrow and tell him I want to see him in a few days to get his time straightened out. McCollister can go to his cabin and bring him out to Headquarters, but he had better go alone. I don't think it would be a good idea for Moreland to see you again so soon. I'm sure he is aware of McCollister's reputation, and I don't think he will make any trouble for Red." The husky McCollister was among the most able men in the woods.

"The poor little son-of-a-bitch," Hansen said. "Somebody must have beaten the hell out of him at one time or another. He's got a bullet scar on one of his ankles. He's had a rough life, but we can't have him causing trouble. I'm going to fire him."

"Let me talk to him first. Maybe I can get him to put his guns away."

"All right, but I think he's got to go."

Hansen telephoned Moreland the next day and told him that Bradbury wanted to see him. Moreland seemed to be in a good mood. On April 22, McCollister returned to Moreland's cabin, again towing a load of lumber behind the bulldozer. When McCollister arrived, he found a calmer man than the suspicious, anxious character who had pulled a gun on Hansen. The Ridgerunner greeted McCollister cordially and readily consented to ride out of the woods with the big lumberjack.

On the way to Camp T, McCollister and Moreland stopped for lunch and built a fire to keep warm. During the meal, McCollister learned that Moreland knew a lot about him, even though he had never seen Moreland until a few days before.

"You used to be the boss in a camp where Hansen worked, didn't you?" Moreland asked.

"Yes, I did," McCollister said.

"But you quit The Potlatch for a while, and when you came back Hansen was your boss, right?"

"That's right." The two men ate in silence for a moment.

"What's gone wrong between you and Hansen?" McCollister asked.

"I've got that big son-of-a-gun's goat, and I'm not going to let it go," Moreland answered.

The next day, Sunday, April 23, Moreland met with Bradbury. It was a long meeting, starting at 11:45 a.m. and lasting all afternoon. Bradbury talked Moreland into leaving his guns at the office in Headquarters, and Moreland agreed to leave the area for good when the fluming was done at the end of the season. He said he was going to the east, and he signed a statement to that effect.

Moreland returned to the bunkhouse in the early evening. He and McCollister were the only two men staying in the bunkhouse that night.

"How did your meeting with Bradbury go?" McCollister asked.

"Fine," Moreland replied. "I told him I wouldn't wear my pistol to work any more. You know, that Bradbury's got a lot of problems, too."

With that, Moreland climbed into an upper berth and went to sleep, still in his clothes.

The next day, Moreland and McCollister returned to Camp T. McCollister said he would give Moreland a ride to the river, but the Ridgerunner insisted that he would walk and took off for his cabin on snowshoes.

Bradbury wanted to give Moreland another chance, but Hansen was adamantly against the idea.

"We've got to think of the other men," Hansen said. "I'm not going to have him around."

"Okay, Fred," Bradbury said. "Fire him if you want to. It's your camp."

Hansen talked to Moreland on the telephone.

"Bill, that's all," Hansen said. "I can't keep you any more."

Moreland picked up his paycheck at Camp T in May. A few days later, he arrived in Headquarters to pick up the guns he had left earlier.

"Are you going to leave for the east, as you said you would?" Bradbury asked.

"No," Moreland replied. "I'm headed for Big Island and Canyon Ranger Station. I'm going to work for the Forest Service."

Bradbury knew that Moreland would never get a job with the Forest Service, and he was exasperated to hear that the little man wasn't leaving.

"You have caused a lot of problems in these mountains," Bradbury said curtly. "You ought to stop causing trouble for others."

Moreland left Headquarters that night, but it wasn't long before his next run-in with PFI. On a rainy night in June, a loud explosion rocked the stillness of Camp T. Hansen jumped out of bed and pulled on his clothes. It sounded as if the explosion came from a nearby landing, where logs were loaded, and Hansen ran in that direction.

The entire camp awoke. The loggers, in undershirts, suspenders, and unlaced boots, walked through a warm, light rain toward the landing, bunching up behind the few men who had thought to bring flashlights.

The blast had blown the engine out of a Caterpillar D-8 bulldozer, a huge, expensive piece of machinery. Flames danced upward from the bulldozer's massive frame; there was nothing Hansen and his men could do. The bulldozer, one of the most costly pieces of equipment PFI owned, was a total loss.

TEN

It seemed obvious that Moreland had destroyed the PFI bulldozer. He had a motive, since Hansen had fired him. He had led a life of crime in the past, and he had problems getting along with others. Perhaps he would take out his anger through a destructive act.

Some Clearwater County residents hoped that Moreland would get away after leading PFI on a merry chase. The company, the biggest firm in north-central Idaho, had its detractors.

The morning after the explosion, deputized men were posted at the bridge across the North Fork near Canyon Ranger Station. Canyon Ranger O.J. Esterol, whose wife was due to deliver a baby, was one of them. The men stopped the few vehicles that came to the bridge, but saw no sign of Moreland.

That same morning, Bradbury, Edelblute, PFI lawyer George Beardmore, and Clearwater County Sheriff V.L. "Slim" Holloway met in Orofino. Representatives of the Clearwater Timber Protective Association and the Forest Service also attended the meeting. It was decided that a concerted effort would be made to catch Moreland.

Bradbury, Edelblute, Beardmore, and the sheriff drove to Camp T that afternoon, arriving at 5:30 p.m. They began their investigation that evening, finding footprints around the wrecked bulldozer. Holloway made plaster casts of the prints.

Early the next morning, Beardmore and Bradbury hiked down the flume and found more footprints and made more casts. Edelblute and Holloway struck out in another direction, walking toward a cabin not far from camp, where they also found footprints and made casts.

The four met back at Camp T at lunch. The sheriff left for town that afternoon. Bradbury and Edelblute followed a set of footprints to a road junction called Bingo Saddle, but saw no sign of Moreland.

Two days later Al Kroll, the assistant camp boss at Camp 60, reported that a man who looked like Moreland had walked through camp about 2:30 in the afternoon. Bradbury called Holloway. The sheriff said he would attempt to run Moreland down.

Holloway and a deputy arrived at Headquarters the next morning with bloodhounds. They rode the PFI rail line to Camp 14, where Camp Boss Whitey Welland drove them on to the Shin Point trail, which cut downhill to the North Fork from Camp 60.

For four days the two lawmen and their dogs tried to pick up Moreland's trail, but had no luck. Holloway suspended the search on July 4. The next day a note written by Moreland was found in a telephone box on the PFI rail line two miles north of Headquarters. Apparently, the little man had been near Headquarters while the sheriff searched for him in the brush.

Two days later, at 9:30 in the morning, Moreland walked into the PFI warehouse at Headquarters. Twelve days had passed since the explosion destroyed the bulldozer.

"I hear you've been looking for me," Moreland said. "I understand that one of your Cats was blown up."

Holloway, who was in Headquarters with a deputy, took Moreland into custody. While the sheriff and his prisoner were preparing to leave, Moreland confided that he had a cache near Camp T. Holloway, Beardmore, and a group of PFI employees accompanied Moreland to Camp T, and Moreland led the group down the flume to his cache.

Moreland stopped at the base of a widowmaker, which is a tree that has fallen part way to the ground before hanging up in the branches of another tree. He walked up the trunk of the widowmaker—a dangerous stunt since it could have come free at any moment—and retrieved a dirty packsack hidden in the branches.

Holloway and Beardmore found a pair of boots in the packsack. One of the lumberjacks who was present had been a captain in the San Francisco

Police Department; he compared the soles of the boots, which had no heels, with the plaster casts Holloway had made of the footprints near the bulldozer. They matched.

Moreland gave Holloway and Beardmore more evidence to use against him. He said he had walked right by the bulldozer the day before it was destroyed.

Moreland's chances of being acquitted looked slim. On July 20, he represented himself in a preliminary hearing in Orofino before Justice of the Peace Charles W. McEachron and did a poor job. Asked by McEachron whether he wanted an attorney, Moreland said, "I see no need for one."

After Clearwater County Prosecuting Attorney Frank Kimble questioned Beardmore, McEachron leaned forward and asked Moreland whether he had any questions to ask the witness.

"Only one damned question," Moreland answered, turning to peer at the witness. "You stated the engine was blown up by dynamite. Did they find any damned papers?"

Kimble tried to interrupt, but Moreland cut him short.

"If you done so much damned investigating, you could have found the papers and fingerprints," he declared.

McEachron interrupted. "Are you asking questions or testifying?" he said.

"I am merely stating where they are damned careless. It is impossible to handle dynamite without leaving fingerprints on the papers."

Moreland also asked Sheriff Holloway, the only other witness in the proceeding, whether he found dynamite papers at the scene. The sheriff said he had not.

"There must have been the yellow wrappers off that dynamite and a person could have left his fingerprints on them," Moreland insisted.

"What was the question?" Holloway asked.

"I don't know that it was a question," the judge observed. "I think it was just a statement."

"I asked him to get all those damned papers, but he didn't get them," Moreland muttered.

The judge admonished Moreland.

"That isn't a question," he said. "You understand you are not on trial in this hearing at all. We are simply here to establish whether a crime was committed and whether there is probable cause to believe that you committed it."

After Holloway was excused, the prosecution rested.

"Is there anything you would like to put before the court?" McEachron asked Moreland. Moreland began, "In 1948, I wrote the state game department that their trappers were crooked..."

"That has nothing to do with this case," McEachron said. "I will have nothing to do with that. You are charged with blowing up an engine of the Potlatch Forests and the game department has nothing to do with that. Have you anything more to say?"

"I almost had a fight up there in the brush," Moreland said, apparently referring to the incident with Hansen.

"That could be brought up at the trial."

Kimble offered to allow Moreland to be sworn in so that he could state his allegations for the record. McEachron agreed. Moreland claimed he had notified the Idaho Fish & Game Department two years earlier that PFI employees had killed elk out of season. He insisted that he had seen two men cook elk meat on the stove at Camp X in the spring of 1948.

He also said that PFI employees had thrown rocks at him, and that he had told Bradbury of the incident. "He jumped up on his hind feet, and I said, 'I can prove it damned shortly,'" Moreland said.

Bradbury threatened to remove him from PFI property, Moreland said. "I have been there five years and they didn't have the nerve to kick me out, and he said, 'We can get you out of there. You wait and watch that.'"

"When was this conversation with Mr. Bradbury when he said he wanted you 'out of there?'" Kimble asked.

"May."

"What year?"

"This year."

Kimble took the opportunity to ask Moreland whether he had been near the bulldozer on either Sunday, June 25th, which was the day before the machine exploded, or early Monday, when the blast went off.

"It was Saturday, Sunday or Monday," Moreland said.

"That is all," Kimble said.

"Any further statement?" the judge asked Moreland.

"That's all I know of," Moreland replied.

McEachron bound Moreland over to District Court for trial and set bail at $5,000, an amount the Ridgerunner could not meet. The trial was to be held before District Judge Albert Featherstone in Orofino on Oct. 17. A week before it began, District Judge Jack McQuade visited Ray McNichols, an Orofino attorney.

Even though he was not scheduled to try the case, McQuade intended to see that Moreland got a fair trial. He knew that McNichols would defend Moreland vigorously.

Unlike some local lawyers, McNichols was not beholden to PFI, even though he had worked on the company's woods crews during summers while in college. McNichols represented Clearwater County against PFI in property-tax equalization hearings; he had never lost to the company in the hearings, in which PFI challenged assessments the county placed on its land. McQuade got right to the point in his conversation with McNichols.

"I want to see that the Ridgerunner gets a fair trial," he said. "He's got some fool notion that he's going to defend himself. Will you take his case, Ray?" McNichols said that he would.

Moreland was released from jail a week before the trial so that he could aid in his defense. He rented a room in the Lumberman's Hotel, which sat across Orofino Creek from the main part of town, and McNichols called on him there. When McNichols knocked on the door, Moreland opened it a crack and glared out suspiciously.

"Who are you?" he said. "Are you with The Potlatch?"

"My name is Ray McNichols, and I've been appointed by the court to act as your attorney," McNichols responded. "May I come in?"

"No," Moreland said. "I don't need an attorney. I'm defending myself."

"Lawyers say that a man who defends himself has a fool for a client. Why don't you let me in and we'll talk about your case?"

Moreland stepped back and opened the door. McNichols entered the room. It was furnished only with a single bunk, a table and a chair. McNichols sat in the chair.

"Now, tell me how you got yourself into this mess," he said.

"It's The Potlatch," Moreland replied. "They're trying to get me out of the woods."

Moreland talked readily, but McNichols could see he was far from an ideal client. He had a know-it-all attitude, was argumentative, and was determined to mastermind his own defense. He claimed that PFI blasting crews discolored streams and killed fish when the company built logging roads, and he wanted to bring that out in court even though it had nothing to do with his case. Moreland seemed to be keenly intelligent, however, and he might make an excellent witness. That was especially true since it was likely the jury would include panelists who had an axe to grind with PFI.

Through discovery, McNichols learned that the prosecution had a good deal of circumstantial evidence, but little physical evidence. McNichols suspected that the charge had been filed before a proper investigation was conducted, perhaps to appease PFI. He was convinced that Moreland had a good chance to beat the rap, and he decided to put Moreland on the stand.

The morning the trial began, spectators streamed into the courtroom. Bradbury, McCollister, Hansen, Edelblute, and six other PFI employees —a total of 11 men who worked for the company—were present. McNichols was glad to see the showing the company made. The jurors might think that PFI was trying to intimidate them and react negatively. Beardmore, PFI's lawyer, sat at the prosecution's table to assist Prosecutor Kimble.

With all but one member of the jury chosen, McNichols finished questioning a prospective juror and turned to ask Moreland if he approved of the juror.

"How about it, Bill," McNichols asked. "Are you satisfied with that jury?"

"I don't like the looks of that fellow with the specs on," Moreland replied.

The spectators laughed, a bespectacled man stepped down from the witness stand, and the bailiff called the name of another panelist.

After the jury was empanelled, Kimble called Sheriff Holloway as the first prosecution witness.

"Sheriff, do you have reason to believe that the defendant was near the bulldozer not long before it was destroyed?" Kimble asked.

"Yes," Holloway responded.

"Please explain."

"Mr. Moreland made a statement to me when I arrested him. He said that he was in the general vicinity northwest of Headquarters the day before the bombing. He said he was at Camp T that day, Sunday the 25th of June."

"Did Mr. Moreland merely say that he was in the vicinity, or did he say that he was near the bulldozer?"

"He said he walked right by that Cat and went over the hill on his way into the woods."

"What time would this have been?"

"He said he was at Camp T between 10 and 2 o'clock, and that he had gone over the hill from there."

"That would have been about 12 hours before the explosion?"

"Yes. According to several people, the explosion went off at 1:45 a.m. on the 26th."

"Did Mr. Moreland make these statements voluntarily?"

"Yes."

The court recessed for the day with Holloway still on the stand. Toward the end of the day's proceedings, Moreland passed a note to Bradbury. "Why are you having your daughter defend you?" the note asked.

Marjorie Bradbury had accompanied her father to court that day. Moreland glared at the girl as she left the courtroom. He scared her, and her mother refused to let her return the next day.

The trial went into full swing in its second day. Kimble called several of the PFI employees, including Beardmore, his co-counsel, to the stand.

"Did you find signs that someone had been near the tractor?" Kimble asked Beardmore.

"Yes, there were definite signs of people being around, or, I should say, of a person being around."

"What were those signs?"

"It had rained that night, and there were footprints near the tractor."

"Did you find other signs nearby that indicated someone had been around?"

"Yes."

"What were those signs?"

"We found a place up on the hill where someone had been in the brush. The spot more or less resembled a nest, with the grass and brush beaten down and empty food tins lying around."

"Do you know whose nest this was?"

"The defendant, Mr. Moreland, is the only person in the area who is known to live like this."

Like Holloway, Beardmore testified that Moreland had said he had walked past the bulldozer the day before the explosion. Kimble continued his questioning, getting on the record Moreland's employment history with PFI—including the fact that the company had fired him.

"Why was Mr. Moreland fired?" Kimble asked.

"He was fired because he pulled a gun during an argument with Fred Hansen, the boss at Camp T."

Kimble questioned Hansen about the incident, then asked Hansen whether Moreland continued to show animosity toward him.

"Yes," Hansen replied.

"Can you give us an example of this?"

"He sits up on the hill above Camp T and fires shots near me with his .22 while I am working."

"How do you know this?"

"He told some of the men. One of them asked him if he was trying to kill me, and he said he just wanted to see how close he could come. I haven't heard the gunshots because a .22 isn't very loud, he shoots from far away, and there's a lot of noise around camp."

"Boots" Edelblute testified that he and Moreland had not gotten along since Moreland gave his paycheck to Bernajean Edelblute.

"Mr. Edelblute, do you still see Mr. Moreland occasionally?" Kimble asked.

"Yes I do."

"And is he cordial?"

"No."

"Please explain."

"I see him while I am in the woods working. He steps out from behind a tree or a rock. He always has his rifle with him. He follows me through the woods for miles sometimes. He also shadows other men who work for PFI. He startles you when he does this. He seems to think it's some sort of game. I don't."

Edelblute, a powerful man who had wrestled in college, easily could have bested Moreland in any physical encounter. Yet he found Moreland's behavior unnerving.

"He's crafty," Edelblute continued. "You never see him coming. He always surprises you."

Kimble introduced into evidence the plaster casts of the footprints found near the bulldozer. He also introduced the boots that Moreland had removed from his cache the day he was arrested. Then Moreland took the stand.

Moreland freely admitted that Hansen fired him and that he harbored ill feelings toward Hansen, Edelblute, and other PFI employees. Then Kimble picked up Moreland's boots and held them in the little man's face.

"Do you own these boots?" Kimble demanded. Moreland wrinkled his nose, closed his eyes and looked away from the boots. Some of the spectators let out muffled laughs.

"Mr. Moreland," Kimble repeated, "are you the owner of these boots?"

Again Moreland made a face and turned his head.

"Your honor, the witness is not answering the question," Kimble said.

"Mr. Moreland, you will answer the question," Judge Featherstone directed.

Moreland opened one eye and looked at the boots.

"I think they're mine," he said. "I don't want to look too closely because they hurt my feet so much."

Muffled laughter was heard again.

"That is not an adequate answer," Kimble persisted. "Are you or are you not the owner of these boots?"

"Well, I've been the owner since I found them in The Potlatch's bunkhouse," Moreland said. "Did you want to know if I was the owner then, or if I am the owner now?"

Several spectators laughed aloud, and Kimble turned to the judge again.

"Your honor, the witness is not limiting himself to answers," Kimble said. "He's answering the question with questions of his own."

"Mr. Moreland, please restrict yourself to answers," the judge said.

"Yes, your honor."

Kimble tried once more.

"Mr. Moreland, are these your boots?" he asked.

"Yes."

"Please tell us, Mr. Moreland, why the heels have been cut out?"

"So I could wear them backwards."

"So you could wear them backwards? Why would you want to wear your boots backwards?"

"To throw people off my trail."

"In other words, you wished to escape detection."

"No law against that, is there?"

Two spectators covered their mouths with their hands to stifle laughs. Kimble paused, then went on.

"Were these boots found in the packsack that you gave to Sheriff Holloway and Mr. Beardmore on the day of your arrest?" he asked.

"Well, I didn't find them there because I knew they were there, but your dear Potlatch friends found them in my packsack."

"Were you wearing the boots on Sunday, June the 25th?"

"I can't remember if I was wearing those contemptible things or not, but I did walk right by that Cat, if that's what you mean. I walked right by it and on over the hill."

"The footprints show that a man not only walked by the Cat, Mr. Moreland, but walked up to it and stood beside it. Did you walk up to the Cat and stand beside it?"

"Yes."

"Were you standing close enough to the Cat to plant dynamite in the engine?"

McNichols objected to the question, but Featherstone let it stand, and Moreland affirmed that he could have put dynamite in the engine compartment from where he stood.

"Why did you stand so close to the bulldozer, Mr. Moreland?" Kimble continued.

"My pack was heavy and I wanted to rest. I backed up to the 'dozer and set my pack on the track."

"And why was your pack so heavy? What did you have in the pack?"
"Rocks."
This time, the entire courtroom erupted into laughter. Featherstone pounded his gavel to quell the outburst.
"I will clear this courtroom if that's what it takes to maintain order," the judge warned.
Kimble was flustered. He noticed that some of the jurors had laughed along with the crowd, and he tried to regroup.
"Mr. Moreland, did you enter the kitchen at the Potlatch Forests camp known as Camp 14 last year?" Kimble asked curtly.
"Yes."
"You admit being inside then?"
"I was inside, although I didn't break in. It's true that the door was locked, but the window was open. I did open the window a little further so I could get through, but I didn't take much. I just took some ginger snaps. I like ginger snaps, you know."
Some of the spectators tittered, but the noise subsided when Featherstone reached for his gavel. The judge set the gavel down without using it; Kimble again took up a new line of questioning.
"Mr. Moreland, you have admitted that you were in the vicinity of the bulldozer the weekend that it was destroyed. Where did you go after you walked by the Cat?"
"I walked up on the hill. I came to a little creek and sat down on a bridge and fed the trout bread crumbs. Then I made a bed for the night."
"Your bed was at the nest the investigators found?"
"Yes."
"And you were at that spot when the Cat blew up?"
"Yes. I was asleep. I heard an explosion and got up and saw that the Cat was on fire."
"What did you do?"
"I had a box of Ritz crackers with me, and I sat down on a rock and ate the crackers and watched the 'dozer burn."
"Mr. Moreland, you have admitted that you were in the vicinity of the bulldozer the night it was destroyed and that you stood right next to the bulldozer just hours before the explosion blew it apart. You testified you were so close to the machine that you set your pack on its tracks. By your own admission you dislike Potlatch Forests Inc. and some of the company's employees. Now you tell us you watched the bulldozer burn, but from afar, and all you were doing was eating Ritz crackers. Doesn't all this prove something?"

"Yes."

"And what is that?"

"It proves I like Ritz crackers."

The courtroom exploded with laughter. A smile flickered across Featherstone's face before he grabbed his gavel.

Kimble, momentarily dumbfounded, met Moreland's gaze. Moreland smiled wickedly. When the laughter died down, Kimble asked one final question.

"So those facts prove that you like Ritz crackers—and that's all?" he said, feigning incredulity.

"Of course," Moreland replied. "I like cookies, too."

Some snickers were heard, but Featherstone looked as if he really would clear the courtroom, and the noise subsided.

As McNichols began his cross-examination, he knew that Moreland had been a far better witness than he had hoped. Moreland had been a perfect foil to the humorless prosecutor and might have won the case.

"Bill," McNichols began, "do you believe that PFI wants you out of the woods?"

"Yes."

"Do you have proof of this?"

"Yes."

"Please explain."

"I went to Headquarters in April to see Bradbury. Bradbury asked me to leave my guns at his office. After I gave him my guns, he asked if I might leave the country. I told him I had thought about going to the east. He wrote out an agreement, saying that I would leave as soon as the fluming was done. I signed the paper; I figured it wasn't legal."

"Did you later tell Mr. Bradbury you had changed your mind?"

"Yes. After I got my last check at Camp T, I went to Headquarters to pick up my guns and talked to Bradbury in his office."

"When was this?"

"In May."

"What did Mr. Bradbury say to you?"

"He asked me if I was going to leave; I told him no."

"What did he say?"

"He got up on his hind legs and shook the paper at me. He said, 'You signed this. You agreed to leave the country. It says so right here.'"

Moreland's statement set the minds of the spectators working. Perhaps PFI really had tried to get the little man out of the woods.

Testimony concluded late that afternoon, and the court scheduled closing arguments for the next morning, the third day of the trial.

In his closing statement, Kimble dwelled on Moreland's run-ins with Bradbury and Hansen and his admission that he stood next to PFI's bulldozer the day before it was destroyed. McNichols told the jury that Moreland should receive credit for being honest about his whereabouts.

"It's not unusual for Mr. Moreland to pass by almost any point in the mountains," McNichols said. "He travels constantly. He has made no secret of the fact that he walked right by the bulldozer hours before the explosion, but that does not mean he blew it up. That statement is a circumstantial piece of evidence.

"This man, you'll remember, has made a life's work out of being in the woods," McNichols continued. "That's why they call him the Ridgerunner. But just because he does not live like you or I or Mr. Kimble or Mr. Bradbury does not mean that he is any more of a criminal than you or I or Mr. Kimble or Mr. Bradbury. Mr. Moreland may have a packrat attitude, and he may be different, but he's not charged with having a packrat attitude or being different. He is charged with blowing up a bulldozer, and the state has an obligation to prove to you, beyond a reasonable doubt, that he blew up that bulldozer. The state has not met its obligation."

In its initial deliberations, the jury leaned toward conviction. On the first ballot, just three members voted for acquittal. One of the three, jury foreman Lavell Beck, made an impassioned plea. He had worked in the woods and used explosives, and his words carried weight with the other jurors.

"The Potlatch witnesses sounded like their testimony was rehearsed," Beck said. "It was just like listening to a record, over and over again."

The prosecution had contended that a knife found in Moreland's packsack had bits of dynamite fuse on the blade, but Beck examined the knife and disagreed.

"That's just plain ordinary rust," he said.

A PFI witness had testified that the explosion sounded as if it were made by 40 percent TNT, a mixture that the company used to blast stumps. Beck said the witness wouldn't have made the comment unless he knew what the mixture was.

"She's all a frame-up," Beck concluded. "I'll stay here till my whiskers drag before I'll believe he's guilty."

The jury broke for lunch, then continued its deliberations until mid-afternoon. Four hours after it went out, it returned. It had found Moreland not guilty.

Moreland was jubilant. He told Sam Swayne, McNichols' law partner, that he would bring the skins of a half dozen martens to the law offices of Swayne & McNichols to pay for his defense. The county paid for McNichol's services, but for years afterward whenever Swayne saw Moreland, Moreland promised to get him "those dear martens." He never did, however.

A week after the trial, Bradbury received a note from Moreland.

"Howard Bradbury, the rat that would use company machinery to haul out your illegal elk meat," the note began. "I heard about your reward, you slim-mouth lying rat."

Bradbury, who had a thin face, had offered no reward. Moreland had signed the note twice, adding the name J.B. Kent to his own signature.

Despite the note's threatening tone, Moreland treated Bradbury cordially when the two met, although he was reserved. He continued to use the company's buildings and supplies at will, as he had before the trial.

One winter day, Wallace Boll, PFI's railroad superintendent at Headquarters, saw Moreland hiking along a road in the woods. It was snowing, and Boll offered Moreland a ride. Moreland accepted, and when Boll dropped him off, he said, "Tell Bradbury I'm going to use his shack for a few days."

"What shack?" Boll asked.

"The shack at the end of the Camp T flume."

Moreland didn't wait for Boll's approval. He jumped down from the pickup, slammed the door and made off through the brush. Boll drove on, bemused but unsurprised.

Not long after the trial, several logs went through the side of the Camp T flume. The logs could not be salvaged, and fluming operations had to be halted for several hours. It appeared that someone had ripped boards out of the side of the flume, allowing the logs to escape. A carpenter found a note nailed to the flume. It read, "Here we have the boss, kind-hearted Fred. He helped the Wobblies lose 1,000 feet of lumber." The Wobblies, the storied Industrial Workers of the World, had struck PFI years before, but had been inactive in the area for years. Hansen was certain that Moreland had written the note.

ELEVEN

After Moreland's acquittal, he returned to the life he had pursued before he was arrested. He worked for a few months at a time, then disappeared into the mountains for long periods.

Just two years passed before he was on trial again. He was charged this time with assault with a deadly weapon. Allegedly, he fired a shot at a man named Arthur Foster, with whom he worked at Studebaker's Mill near Pierce.

The prosecution's case was strong. That became apparent during Moreland's preliminary hearing before Judge McEachron on Aug. 28, 1952. Millwright Charles Stevenson had seen Moreland fire the shot, and he testified for the prosecution during the hearing. Moreland and Foster worked on pieces of equipment just eight feet apart that day, and Moreland left the mill at 5 o'clock as usual, Stevenson said.

"When did you next see him?" Prosecutor Warren F. Gardner asked the witness.

"In about 15 minutes."

"Would you describe what you noticed about Mr. Moreland?"

"He had a holster strapped on."

"Did he have the holster on when he left the mill?"

"No, sir."

"What did Mr. Moreland do?"

"He turned and faced Arthur Foster."

"How close to Mr. Moreland was Mr. Foster?"

"About 11 feet."

"Then what happened, Mr. Stevenson?"

"He pulled out a revolver and fired a shot."

"Did you notice what type of revolver it was?"

"It was a .22."

"Could you tell what he was shooting at?"

"The gun was pointing in the general direction of Foster."

"Did Mr. Moreland say anything?"

"He fired the shot first, and then he spoke."

"What did he say?"

"He said, 'Art, you are all through working. Get out of this mill and get a gun and we will fight it out like a man.' Then Art said, 'Are you crazy? What's the matter, Shorty, are you crazy?' Then he repeated that two or three times."

"Then what happened?"

"Moreland accused him of telling Mr. Studebaker things."

"Mr. Studebaker is the owner of the mill?"

"Yes."

"In what position was the revolver held by Mr. Moreland while this conversation took place?"

"At Mr. Foster."

"Aimed at Mr. Foster?"

"Aimed in that direction."

Gardner turned the witness over to Moreland's attorney, Ray McNichols. Moreland had a reputation for being a crack shot, and McNichols tried to use it to his client's advantage.

"Are you acquainted with Mr. Moreland's reputation for accuracy with a gun?" he asked Stevenson.

"No, sir."

"You have never heard anyone say he was a good shot?"

"No, sir."

"You say he was about 11 feet away from Mr. Foster?"

"Yes."

"Would you say a man familiar with firing a weapon, as Mr. Moreland is, would hit a man at 11 feet?"

Gardner jumped to his feet before Stevenson could answer.

"I object," he said. "That calls for a conclusion."

"Sustain the objection," the judge said. "I don't think he is an expert on firearms."

"From the position, the angle, you were standing at, could you tell for sure whether Mr. Moreland was shooting at Mr. Foster?" McNichols asked.

"It looked like the gun was pointed right at him."

Stevenson testified that Moreland was disarmed after Gilbert Studebaker, the mill owner, fired a shot to attract his attention. Stevenson's testimony was damning, and at the conclusion of the hearing, McEachron ordered Moreland bound over to District Court to stand trial.

"The court feels that under the statute, the intent was there," McEachron said.

Moreland, who could not meet his $1,000 bail, was jailed to await trial. Moreland's trial was scheduled for October. In the interim, a psychiatrist named R.H. Southcombe examined him. Moreland told Southcombe many things that varied with statements he had made earlier. For instance, he told the doctor he had been born in Minnesota, rather than Kentucky.

"I don't know much about my father," Moreland said. "I believe he was a revenue agent and was shot. I don't know much about my mother, either." Moreland had said earlier that his mother was dead.

Moreland claimed that his schooling ended after he finished the eighth grade in Minnesota. Earlier, he had said he went through the fifth grade in Kentucky.

Southcombe wrote in his report that Moreland moved to Missouri when he was 17 to attend mining school.

"He became friendly with a family in Missouri and ran away with their 15-year-old daughter and was married by a Justice of the Peace," the doctor said. "He relates that when they returned the marriage was annulled and the girl was placed in a convent."

Moreland claimed that he stopped an attempt to dynamite a bank building in Arkansas where he worked as a custodian. He denied that he was sentenced in the incident.

Moreland told the doctor he moved to Montana from Arkansas and spent 12 years prospecting in the Bitterroot Mountains, where his use of government cabins and supplies led to run-ins with the Forest Service. From Montana, he said he went to Idaho and worked as a woodsman. He confided he had trouble with other men in the woods camps where he worked.

"He relates circumstances relative to two recent events," Southcombe wrote.

"It appears that his working partner became acutely ill requiring hospitalization and, basing an opinion on incomplete reports, Moreland expressed the opinion that he had been poisoned; he relates in detail circumstances occurring in a camp where he was charged with operating an electric generator. Following orders, he shut the generator off when the lights were no longer required in the cook shack; an office employee started the generator in order to supply electricity for his radio. Moreland again shut off the generator. It was restarted and Moreland then turned the generator on to capacity and burned up the radio."

Moreland told Southcombe that Foster had called him a "punk," and he talked about his arrest in 1950, "when the 'dozer broke up."

He described himself as a woodsman, denied excessive use of alcohol and said he did not use narcotics at all. "He states that he does not associate with women, that he has no interest in them because he still remembers the girl whom he married in his youth," Southcombe wrote.

The report continued, "Moreland relates the story of his adult life living in the woods, depending upon himself, and emphasizes the pleasure he derived from observing wild animals in their natural habitat. He describes a bobcat which he raised and remarks that...he finds it difficult to mingle with adults."

Southcombe found no "gross memory defects" and no evidence of delusion. He said Moreland was in good contact with reality and possessed a "native intelligence."

The psychiatrist added these comments:

"The history indicates that this man was practically abandoned by his family and lived in orphanages during the important formative years. In his youth there was no occupational stability and on at least two occasions he became involved in difficulty with the law. After moving to the west he has lived practically a solitary existence apparently finding recreation in the simple activity of his immediate environment—indicated by his interest in animals.

"He is apparently unable to adjust to adult society, and in my opinion, it may be reasonable to assume that because of the unsatisfactory environment of his boyhood and youth he entertains some hostility toward society, and because he has no adult associates with whom he may take counsel he resorts to detailed reports concerning misconduct in others."

Southcombe continued, "This man, in my opinion, exhibited a distorted personality, not, however, to a degree justifying the diagnosis, 'psychopathic personality.' His querulous attitude is the most important aspect of this personality distortion."

Southcombe concluded that Moreland was sane and capable of recognizing his legal jeopardy and aiding in his own defense. Southcombe finished his report on Oct. 20, eight days before the trial; Judge Jack McQuade, who would sit in the case, ruled the next day that the trial could go forward.

Moreland was up against a shrewd and capable adversary in Gardner. McQuade, who again was determined that Moreland would get a fair trial, asked Moreland a number of times if he was sure he wouldn't have an attorney. Moreland said that he was sure.

During breaks in the one-day trial, Moreland sat on the courthouse steps reading a pocketbook, seemingly unconcerned about the outcome.

After the closing arguments, jury foreman Gerald Millard summed up his thoughts for his fellow jurors.

"I wish that the defendant had been represented by an attorney," Millard said. "An attorney would have brought out some of the points he tried to bring out, but done a better job of it. He didn't deny firing the shot, and there's only one way we can vote on this, as I see it."

The jury reached a verdict within an hour, and Millard announced to the court that Moreland had been found guilty.

McQuade told Moreland that assault with a deadly weapon was a serious offense.

"Even though you claim that you were merely trying to frighten Arthur Foster, and you say that you had been taunted by him, there is no excuse for your act," McQuade went on.

"You were in no danger when you armed yourself and confronted Mr. Foster, so self-defense does not enter in. As well, the bullet you fired might have struck another person.

"Even though your combativeness toward Mr. Foster might have been understandable, no court can or should overlook the seriousness of your actions. This court hopes that the punishment it metes out will help you use restraint if such a situation arises again."

McQuade paused and shuffled through a sheaf of papers that lay before him on the bench.

"Mr. Moreland," he said, "you have been in trouble before, once for breaking into a store and once for, let me see..."

"I stole a halter," Moreland said. McQuade looked up from his papers.

"It says here you went to prison. You went to prison for stealing a halter?"

"Yes, your honor. There was a horse in it."

The courtroom exploded with laughter. McQuade was momentarily dumbstruck. His hand froze in mid-air, grippng a piece of paper he had picked up before Moreland spoke. Then a smile slowly spread across his face.

"Mr. Moreland, your sense of humor has not been lost on this court," McQuade said. "It is a quality in you that gives this court hope that you can live a fruitful life from now on. First, however, you must pay your debt to society. Do you have anything to say before I sentence you?"

"Thank you for seeing that I got a fair trial, your honor."

"You are welcome, Mr. Moreland. I hereby sentence you to six months in the county jail. Court is adjourned."

Moreland did not serve his full six-month sentence. McQuade freed him a month early, on March 31, 1953. The time off was for good behavior.

TWELVE

After Moreland was released from jail, he moved into an abandoned homesteader's cabin at the mouth of Milk Creek. The cabin, located six miles down the North Fork from Canyon, had no floor and was in bad repair. Moreland slapped cedar shakes over the holes in the roof and walls, but made no attempt to keep the place clean. He called the hovel the "Milk Creek Sub-Station," and he dubbed himself the "acting agent." Moreland erected a slender aspen log in front of his cabin and flew an American flag from the log. He didn't bother to peel the white bark before setting the log in the ground.

Clearwater National Forest Supervisor Fred Stillings saw no point in provoking Moreland. When Stillings assumed his position in 1951, he decided the best way to handle Moreland was to play it low key. He advised his rangers to go about their work and not spend time trying to trap the Ridgerunner.

"Be alert to any activities by Moreland that affect the Forest Service, make a record of them, but take no action to haul him into court for petty offenses," Stillings said. "If brought to trial, it's all too likely he would be turned loose because the offense is minor or we don't have enough evidence or both."

Stillings suggested that employees leave cameras and guns at the ranger stations, where someone was always on duty during fire season. As a result, losses were minimal and in his judgment didn't warrant arresting Moreland.

Moreland could no longer find a job. He pestered J. Frank Meneely, the ranger at Pierce, to hire him. Meneely, whom Moreland called "the dear little ranger," told Moreland he would not hire him. That didn't stop Moreland from asking, though he did so in a cordial way.

Moreland supported himself by growing a big garden, fishing, hunting, gathering berries, and panning gold. As always, his way of life interested the outdoors-minded people of the logging towns.

Louie Jacobsen, a logger from Coeur d'Alene, and three companions visited Moreland at Milk Creek while hiking up the North Fork on a fishing trip.

As the four men came up to the dilapidated building, Moreland was digging feverishly in his garden. He didn't see Jacobsen and his companions until they spoke, which seemed to embarrass him and make him talkative.

"I'm after a mole," he explained, churning away with his shovel. "He's been digging up my garden. If I get him, I'm going to have him for breakfast between two hotcakes."

"Would you mind if I took your picture?" Jacobsen said.

"Being as you asked, I'll let you," Moreland said. "Most people try to get a picture of me, but they don't ask. I don't let many people take my picture. Just a minute and I'll go get Old Glory."

Moreland disappeared into his shack and returned in a moment with an American flag, which had been stored in the accepted triangular fold. While Jacobsen snapped away with his camera, Moreland raised the flag. Jacobsen and his companions were surprised to see that the flag was new.

After he hoisted the flag, Moreland stood beside the flagpole, puffing on his pipe and posing, apparently unaware that Jacobsen had already shot two pictures. Jacobsen snapped his camera a third time.

Jacobsen and his companions left shortly, but saw Moreland when they made their way back down the river that afternoon. Moreland had caught a huge squawfish, which he said he was going to eat for dinner. Since the North Fork was a superabundant trout stream, Jacobsen and his friends couldn't understand why the Ridgerunner would settle for a squawfish. They said nothing, however. The little man wore a pistol on his hip, and they were familiar with his unpredictable nature.

Despite the sympathy with which Moreland was viewed, his reputation made people uneasy. He often brought a firearm when he came to town, and he carrried a rifle as he crossed Pierce's main street one morning and walked toward the Headquarters Cafe. A group of women were in the cafe chatting over coffee as Moreland approached. One of the women looked out the door and said, "Oh God, here comes the Ridgerunner." All conversation ceased as Moreland approached the restaurant. Moreland walked in, stood his rifle upright in a corner and sat down at a table with his back to the gun. As he ordered, the other customers resumed talking.

Moreland's quirks were widely discussed. One story had it that he carried two packsacks when he traveled to town. He was said to tote one of the bags until he came to a bend in the road, then leave it while he went back for the other packsack. He lugged the second bag past the spot where he had left the first, conveying his belongings for miles while keeping both packsacks where he could see them.

Moreland continued to avoid contact with woods travelers. One morning, Forest Service workers John McCluskey and Frank Bringman drove past Moreland, who was walking along a road outside Headquarters. Bringman slammed on the brakes, but by the time he stopped the truck, Moreland had disappeared into the brush.

The little man still obtained the things he needed from the woods camps and Forest Service stations. One of his victims, a lookout in the Bungalow Ranger District, washed his clothes in a creek and stretched them out to dry in the sun. When he returned, his clothes were gone. He ran back to his tower to find that food had been taken.

Panic-stricken, he telephoned the ranger station. He refused to walk out of the woods alone. The ranger had to hike in and and accompany him. He agreed to return to his tower only when the ranger sent another crew member along.

Occasionally, one of Moreland's well-disguised shelters turned up in the woods. In one case, a PFI worker sat on a big cedar stump and dislodged carefully placed pieces of bark before realizing that the stump was a shelter. In another case, a Forest Service worker came upon a cache of canned food and other items near Chateau Rock above Bungalow Ranger Station.

Moreland continued his feud with Frank Marquette, the old prospector whom he had victimized with his thievery before he was captured in 1945. The white-haired Marquette once told Howard Bradbury that Moreland had used his cabin without permission. Marquette said he was going to kill Moreland the next time he saw him. Bradbury asked Marquette later if he had dealt with Moreland. "I ran into him, but I didn't kill him," Marquette said sheepishly. "He traded me out of my rifle. He gave me a pocket watch for it."

Like Moreland, Marquette was a man of some notoriety. Since before Congress created the Clearwater National Forest in 1907 he had sought gold in the North Fork's tributaries, and he lived year-round on his mining claim. Marquette Creek, which ran through the claim, was named after him. Marquette was said to have stomped a path through deep snow over the St. Joe-Clearwater Divide before the turn of the century, enabling a band of starving elk to cross the divide and find food on the Clearwater side. Those elk were said to be the forerunners of the Clearwater herd, but it is unknown whether the story is true.

In 1954, when he was 92, Marquette broke his leg. As he was carried out of the woods on a stretcher, he protested that he could not leave. "I've still got a score to settle with Bill Moreland," he argued.

When his leg mended, Marquette returned to his claim to find a note from Moreland inside his cabin.

The note read:

"Mr. Frank Marquette: "Kind old man, please understand why I stayed at your little cabin. Remember you said there was more shells for the .35. I could not find any. Found three silver dollars and a pocket knife in your bed. Hid them until you come out again."

Moreland placed himself at odds with many others. Crude, hand-painted signs attacking Dwain Space, Moreland's boss with the Potlatch Timber Protective Association, were put up in campgrounds. The signs read, "When Dwain Space asks for your fire permit, do your country a service by asking who gave him a permit to kill game out of season." Space, who had gone out of his way to help Moreland, laughed off the incident as he had laughed off signs that Moreland put up when he worked for the PTPA.

Moreland also wrote letters accusing officials of wrongdoing and sent them to Idaho Gov. Len B. Jordan, the Forest Service, and others. He claimed that while he was a prisoner in the Clearwater County Jail a law enforcement officer raped a girl in a room adjoining the cellblock. Nothing came of the allegation, although he wrote of it repeatedly in his letters.

Moreland frequently mailed his letters in Forest Service envelopes—which bore the legend "Penalty for Private Use." He left some of his letters dangling from strings tied to tree branches; they hung out over the trail where forest travelers would see them. Other letters were found in Forest Service buildings.

Many men received surprise messages from Moreland while they went about their jobs in the forest. Del Cox, who worked at Bungalow Ranger

Station in the 1950s, arrived at the Flat Creek Cabin to find the food cellar had been cleaned out. Moreland had left a note inside the cabin claiming he had seen Cox throw the food over a cliff. "This kind of wastefulness won't be tolerated any longer," warned Moreland's note, which was written on a piece of brown paper sack. Cox thought the note was humorous, but there was little humor in some of Moreland's writings.

Moreland charged that two lookouts employed by the Clearwater Timber Protective Association had elk meat in their possession after hunting season. When he tried to report the incident over the CTPA's telephone network, the lookouts "put the phone out of commission," Moreland charged.

He said he canned as much of the meat as possible and buried the cans near a lookout tower. He claimed in a letter that an agency employee "has been guarding the place and telling people that if I showed up he was going to take a shot at me. Ask him to come down the river this summer. I have some information about his wife and one of the blister rust kids. Tell him to bring his gun along."

The head of the CTPA, Bert Curtis, was a particular target of Moreland's. In one of his letters, Moreland wrote, "Would you mind asking the big loudmouth Bert Curtis why he requested his pets to put the telephone out of commission when the writer endeavored to put a call through to Orofino regarding the 70 pounds of elk meat?"

One of Moreland's allegations finally attracted attention. In March of 1954, he claimed that the Forest Service was poisoning elk near Canyon Ranger Station. The story was reported in an area newspaper and picked up by a news service and run across the country. As soon as it broke, Fred Stillings telephoned Chuck Kern, the assistant Canyon ranger, at Pierce.

"He said we're poisoning the elk in at Canyon," Stillings said. "Meet Homer Stratton at Camp 60 and get in there and see what this is all about."

"I'll get down there in the morning," Kern said.

"Get down there in the morning, hell," Stillings said. "You be there in the morning."

Like Kern, the Ridgerunner was in Pierce that day. The first thing Kern did when he put down the phone was look up Moreland. He found the little man at the Pierce Hotel, where he usually stayed when he came to town.

"You knew we put out elk carcasses laced with 1080 to poison coyotes last spring," said Kern. "There were signs posted around the carcasses warning people to leave them alone, but we picked those carcasses up last fall. What is this elk-poisoning business all about?"

"I saw dead elk out there this winter with porcupine blocks in their mouths," Moreland said. The Forest Service used porcupine blocks, hollow wooden blocks filled with salt and strychnine, to poison porcupines, which gnawed at the floor joists of the agency's buildings. Moreland knew what the blocks were used for, and Kern was certain that Moreland's story was false; still, the Forest Service had little choice but to check it out. Moreland had spent the winter in the mountains; the rangers hadn't.

"Okay," Kern told Moreland. "We'll go look."

Kern, Canyon Ranger Homer Stratton, and game warden Mel Francis were driven to the headwaters of a stream called Teepee Creek. From there, they skied downhill toward Canyon. They had a 75-mile trip ahead of them before they would be flown out of the woods from an airstrip near Perd Hughes' compound.

During their trek, the three men found 14 dead elk, which was not an unusually high number. Many of the big animals died each year when deep snow made browse hard to find and weakened animals fell prey to predators. It was nature's way of thinning the herd.

Stratton, Kern, and Francis had been instructed to obtain stomach samples from dead elk, but the liquids and gases that seeped from the animals' bloated bellies made Kern and Francis ill. Only Stratton could fight back his revulsion sufficiently to perform the task, and it fell to him.

When the three men arrived at Canyon, they found several letters written by Moreland. Kern shook his head as he read the letters.

"You know," he said, "I think Moreland cooked up this cock-and-bull story so we would hike in here and pick up these letters. He probably forgot them when he came out of the woods."

"I think you're right," Stratton said.

It was obvious that Moreland had spent considerable time at the ranger station that winter. Every lock at the station looked as if it had been picked.

Having completed their grisly chore of examining the dead elk, Kern, Stratton and Francis were in high spirits when they left the ranger station. As they approached Perd Hughes' compound, Kern and Stratton teased Francis, who had a reputation as a hard-nosed game warden.

"Are you going to write the Forest Service up for poisoning elk, Mel?" Kern asked.

"How about Chuck and I, Mel?" Stratton said. "Those elk were dead when we found them, you know."

Francis took the ribbing well. It was the sort of kidding that a game warden heard much of in a county like Clearwater, where almost every man and boy had a hunting license.

The needling, however, took on a new pointedness when the three men reached Hughes' place. An old lumberjack known as "One-Eyed Swede" lived at Hughes' lodge that winter. After the Swede let Kern, Francis, and Stratton in, Francis asked where Hughes was.

"Oh, he's down at the river fishing," the Swede said.

A pained look came over Francis's face. Trout season wouldn't be open for another two months; if Hughes were fishing, he was breaking the law.

"Are you going to arrest Perd, Mel?" Kern said. "He might throw us out in the snow if you do. Would you rather write a ticket or sleep inside where it's warm?"

Kern and Stratton laughed, but the Swede, realizing his gaffe, looked at Francis nervously. Francis knew that Kern and Stratton would never let him live it down if he didn't cite Hughes. He also knew they would never let him live it down if they all had to sleep in the snow. Hughes solved Francis's dilemma. He had the good sense to leave his fishing pole at the river.

The tests of the elk stomach samples showed no sign of poison, but Stratton and Francis did not let the matter drop. They tried to persuade Judge McQuade to revoke Moreland's probation and have him arrested. The man had made no attempt to hide his use of the ranger station. He was so brazen as to leave a note full of his ramblings tacked to the door; it was addressed "to any passerby."

Stratton, Kern, and Francis also had found items from Canyon in a cabin down the river owned by a man named Joe Clukey. Moreland said the cabin was abandoned, but Clukey told Stratton that Moreland had made himself at home without permission and had done so in the past. Stratton told the judge that Moreland was a nuisance.

"We have evidence that he spent the winter at Canyon and at Joe Clukey's cabin," Stratton said. "Isn't he still under the court's jurisdiction in the Foster case?"

"Yes," McQuade said. "He is on 18 months' probation, and he still has six months to go."

"He's threatened people in Pierce and Orofino," Stratton continued. "While we were at Canyon checking on his phony elk-poisoning report, we picked up some of his letters. Two of them made threats. He might be dangerous."

"I don't think so," McQuade replied, "and neither did the psychiatrist who examined him before his trial."

McQuade refused to revoke Moreland's probation; it looked like the Forest Service was going to have to put up with the man. Stratton wrote a memorandum to warn his fellow rangers that Moreland would continue to be in the woods. He sent copies of the memo to the St. Joe and Nez Perce forests and to the FBI.

"At last report Moreland was armed with both a rifle and a sidearm," Stratton wrote. "His present location is unknown except that he has gone back into the woods. It is presumed he will continue to roam the North Fork of the Clearwater and the Little North Fork as that is his favorite territory."

Stratton's prediction was correct. Moreland continued to visit Canyon, both when no one was around and during the work season, when he spun stories for the college students who came for summer jobs. His yarns about the "dear rangers" made a big impression on the youths, who had heard all about the Ridgerunner.

Moreland also told Stratton some of his stories. He said that walking across the ice-covered North Fork in the winter and navigating the runoff-swollen river on crude rafts in the spring were the most dangerous things he had ever done. He recalled that he had almost drowned in the river.

Stratton noticed that Moreland never looked anyone in the eye and had a droll way of speaking. The ranger, however, got along with Moreland. He brought the little man tobacco from town, and Moreland appreciated it.

Moreland often passed by the ranger station when he headed upriver to fish and pick huckleberries. When he returned, his packsack was full of the dark blue berries; his unwrapped fish were on top of the berries.

Moreland continued to find a friend in Perd Hughes. Hughes, who religiously chewed Copenhagen snuff in one jaw and Days Work plug tobacco in the other, was known for his tolerance, and Moreland remained welcome at his lodge even after he told the Idaho Fish & Game Department that Hughes had poached a deer and buried the animal's remains in his garden.

Still, Moreland and Hughes had disputes. Moreland angered Hughes by setting wire snares in the hills for deer. Hughes thought the snares were a cruel way to kill animals and tore them out. Moreland fired shots in the direction of Hughes' lodge from the hillside above. Hughes answered the gunfire with shots of his own, firing into the side of the hill.

When Moreland visited Hughes' lodge, moodiness sometimes descended on him, and he grabbed his possessions and stalked off at a moment's notice. It seemed to Ron Hughes, Perd's nephew, that Moreland became irascible when he had been off in the woods by himself.

The boy, who stayed with his uncle for weeks every summer, came to know Moreland well, and Perd told his newphew stories that Moreland had told him. They were wonderful yarns, and the boy realized that men didn't exchange such stories unless they had a good relationship, no matter what the outside appearance.

"Bill says he uses stilts with elk feet on them to throw people off his trail," the elder Hughes told his nephew. "He walks around on the stilts in mud wallows, going in every direction and leaving plenty of tracks. Then he heads off through the brush and hides the stilts."

It was a fascinating, if not quite believable, tale; Ron Hughes heard it elsewhere as he grew up.

Moreland told Perd that he used wire to pull his teeth when they hurt him. He said he tied a wire to the troublesome tooth and to a sapling, which he would bend and let go.

Ron Hughes' visits to the North Fork, which began when he was 10, came at a good time. The river was still untamed, and he fished it every day. One day he hooked 32 cutthroat trout between 12 and 16 inches in length without moving from the rock where he made his first cast.

The men who visited the lodge told the boy stories about gold-panning, logging, and hunting. One of the old lumberjacks, a one-eyed Norwegian named Pete, called elk "el-uh-kees" and talked incessantly of the animals.

Several of the old woodsmen drank heavily. One of them, "Silent Joe" Clukey, was one of Perd's neighbors; he split his time between two old cabins on the river, one a quarter mile upstream from Perd's place and the other five miles farther on, which made him Moreland's neighbor. He had trouble keeping Moreland out of his cabins.

Clukey, who paid no attention to the clouds of mosquitoes that drove other inhabitants of the river crazy, disliked Moreland intensely. He told Ron Hughes, "If he comes around here, I'll shoot him in the butt."

Clukey showed up at Perd's place one afternoon after a trip to Elk River. He had bought three fifths of liquor in town and drained two of them on the way back. He was impossibly drunk, and Ron and Perd helped him walk the quarter mile to the nearest of his cabins. The next day, Ron walked up the river to check on Clukey and found him dead. Silent Joe was stretched out on a sleeping bag, stark naked. His body was covered with hundreds of bug bites. Three hundred dollars in $20 bills lay on the table in his cabin. It appeared that he had drunk himself to death.

One summer Ron brought a new .22-caliber target rifle to the woods. He was showing his uncle the gun when Moreland arrived. As usual, the little man was packing two rifles, one a combination .22-caliber rifle and .410 gauge shotgun, the other a .30-.30 Winchester.

"Look at this gun, Bill," Perd said, showing the Ridgerunner his nephew's rifle. "It's made especially for target shooting."

"I will, but first I want to show this boy some real color," Moreland said. He pulled a poke from his pocket and emptied a small pile of gold flakes into Ron's outstretched hand.

"It took a lot of panning to get that much gold," Moreland said.

The boy had seen much bigger piles of gold, but he played along, pushing the tip of his index finger through the pile of flakes as he examined them.

"There's color there, all right," he said.

"You bet there is," Moreland said.

Ron poured the gold back into Moreland's bag, then Moreland held the boy by the wrist and dusted off his palm into the bag to make sure he got all of the flakes.

"Let's get it all back in the bag," Moreland said with mock seriousness in a scene they both had acted out before. "Now, let's see that rifle," Moreland said.

The little man examined the rifle carefully while Perd explained that its heavy barrel and stock were designed to reduce shake and improve aim.

"It looks like a good gun," Moreland said. "I'll tell you what. I'll bet I can outshoot you, Ron. I'll put my .22-.410 up against your target rifle, one shot apiece and the winner keeps both rifles."

At first, the boy refused, but Moreland insisted, and finally Ron agreed to the shooting contest. Perd affixed a target to an empty five-gallon can and set it against the bank of a road that ran behind Perd's lodge.

Ron, who had the first shot, used the back fence as a rest. As he looked through the telescopic sight of his target rifle, he knew that the contest was unfair. Moreland's weapon had neither a scope nor a special stock and barrel. Still, Moreland was a crack shot, and the boy carefully lined up the cross-hairs of his scope and held his breath, as marksmen are taught to do, when he fired. The rifle cracked, and the boy and the two men ran to the target, which was about 40 yards away.

"He's in the bull's eye; he's right near the middle," Perd said. The boy's shot had hit in the black of the bull's eye, almost dead center. It was a fine shot.

"Let's see if I can do better," Moreland said.

Moreland was cool as he walked back to the firing line. Then he threw his gun to his shoulder and squeezed off a round quickly. He had taken but a moment to fire, and he had not used the fence for a rest. The two men and the boy ran back to the target, and Perd picked it up.

"I think he's got you, Bill," Perd said, showing Moreland the target.

"You're right," Moreland said. "I guess I can't outshoot that target rifle."

Moreland's round had punctured the target near the edge of the bull's eye, just inside the black. His shot was a fine shot, too, especially considering the disadvantages that he had competed under.

"That's a good rifle you've got, Ron," Moreland said, "and now you've got another one." He handed his gun to the youth, his face the picture of good sportsmanship. In the years that followed, Ron never heard Moreland complain about the contest.

THIRTEEN

The truce that the Forest Service had observed with Moreland ended in June of 1954 when Ralph Space replaced Fred Stillings as supervisor of the Clearwater forest. Space, the brother of Dwain Space, read up on Moreland as soon as he moved into his new job. He regarded Moreland as a thorn in the side and estimated it cost the Forest Service a thousand dollars a year to support the man. Space started working to get Moreland committed to the State Hospital North, an institution in Orofino for the mentally ill.

Shortly after Space came to the Clearwater, he went on an annual raft trip down the North Fork organized by Bert Curtis to give high-ranking state officials a look at the Clearwater country's timber stands.

Attorney General Robert E. Smylie and State Superintendent of Public Instruction Elton Jones, who were along on the trip, said that they wanted to meet the Ridgerunner. Curtis was against the idea, but agreed to swing the rafts in to shore when they reached Milk Creek.

As the boats neared Moreland's hovel, two shots rang out and bullets skipped across the water upstream. Curtis was infuriated. He jumped from his raft and bulled through the shallows to the bank. The rest of the party stayed in the boats. As Curtis stormed ashore, Moreland came out from behind a row of cornstalks in his garden.

"What did you fire those shots for?" Curtis roared. "What the hell do you think you're doing?"

"I didn't fire any shots," Moreland said. "My gun is broken. The firing pin came out and I lost it in the grass."

"You fired those shots," Curtis retorted. "Do you know who's out there? The attorney general of Idaho, that's who, and the state superintendent of schools. The attorney general is probably going to be the next governor. You might have hit him or the superintendent."

"You're wrong," Moreland replied. "My gun is broken. It won't fire."

"Why do you keep writing threatening letters to people who work for the association?" Curtis demanded.

"I haven't threatened anyone."

"You wrote a letter to my office that said we'd better come armed the next time we came to see you."

"I thought you had burned down my cabin a mile down the river. I found out that 'Silent Joe' Clukey did it."

"That wasn't your cabin, that was Silent Joe Clukey's cabin," Curtis said.

Moreland shifted from one foot to the other, but said nothing.

"You may have a gun, but I don't think you have the guts to use it," Curtis said. Curtis, who towered above Moreland, grabbed Moreland's revolver out of his hand, broke it open and emptied the cartridges from the gun, dropping them at Moreland's feet.

Two of the cartridges were spent. It was obvious Moreland had fired the shots that skipped across the water. Curtis handed the pistol back to Moreland and stomped away to rejoin his guests.

As the rafts pulled back into the current, a member of the rafting party saw Moreland take a firing pin out of his pocket and screw it back into place in the hammer of his revolver. He wore a second pistol on his hip, but had not unholstered it.

A mile downstream from Moreland's shack, Curtis went ashore and found that a fire had leveled Silent Joe Clukey's cabin. After the rafting party got back to town, Dwain Space told his brother that Clukey had burned the cabin to keep Moreland from using it.

In Curtis, who was the mayor of Orofino, and Ralph Space, Moreland had made two powerful enemies, and he did nothing to ease the tension between himself and the two officials.

Curtis's name was written on a piece of paper attached to the fur of a dead bobcat left hanging over the trail along the North Fork. Bobcats were regarded as vermin then, and Moreland was blamed for the insult.

Moreland said that Space was married to a black woman—in fact,

Space's wife was a Norwegian blonde—and Space was deeply offended. His dislike of Moreland grew when he heard that Moreland referred to him as "Blackie" Space and "Old Horse Face."

Space was a devoted outdoorsman, and Moreland's claim that the Forest Service poisoned elk also offended him. Space had far too much regard for wildlife to be involved in such a deed.

Moreland continued to make the allegation even after Kern, Stratton, and Francis went into the woods to disprove it. In a letter to the Forest Service dated March 7, 1955, he wrote:

"I will offer a suggestion which I believe will strengthen any interested person's belief that unprincipled people could and did throw poison from a plane flying down the river sometime the past February. I was sawing a tree out of the trail when a beautiful elk came staggering and falling down through the rocks and brush, coming to rest flat on its back in the trail about 50 feet from where I am working. At first I tried to turn her over on her belly thinking maybe she could get up. It did not work out so I climbed up the cliff until I found where she started her fall."

Moreland claimed he found a paper sack lodged in the top of a small tree where the elk had fallen. He said a jar had gone through the bottom of the sack when it lodged in the tree; he reasoned that a jar full of poison had been dropped from an airplane. In another letter, Moreland said he came upon an elk that foamed at the mouth after being poisoned. He claimed the animal stood still while he wiped its slavering muzzle.

A year after Space became Clearwater forest supervisor, a young ranger named Floyd Cowles succeeded Homer Stratton at Canyon. The Canyon district was little different in 1955 than it had been in 1942, when Moreland made his first known theft in the Clearwater forest. Vast areas of the district still were without roads, and few people came. The road to Canyon was as rough as ever. Cowles knocked the oil pan off his new Packard Clifford the first time he drove the car over the road, and it had to be towed to Pierce behind a four-wheel-drive Dodge Power Wagon, which barged through mudholes with all four wheels throwing muck against the windshield of Cowles' car. It was almost impossible for Cowles to see so that he could steer.

When Cowles was preparing to burn an old cabin, he first saw the Ridgerunner. Cowles had just finished soaking the floorboards of the building with kerosene when a crewman told him that Moreland was outside.

"I might as well get this over with," Cowles said. He went outside.

The old cabin sat a short distance from the bridge that spanned the North Fork. Moreland stood in the middle of the gray, steel-girder bridge with his hand resting on the rail of the walkway. He cradled his rifle in his other arm and wore a pistol on his hip. He appeared just as he had been described to Cowles, unshaven, disheveled and dirty, looking as if he had been in the woods for years.

"You must be Bill Moreland," Cowles said, offering his hand as he walked up. "I'm Floyd Cowles, the new Canyon ranger."

"Proud to know you," Moreland said. He did not shake Cowles hand, and Cowles let his hand drop.

"Why are you going to burn that cabin?" Moreland asked.

"The supervisor wants to burn it because it gets vandalized so much," Cowles said.

"You mean Old Horse Face?" Moreland said. "How would he know whether it gets vandalized? He never comes out here."

The two men eyed each other for a moment.

"It seems to me if you burn a cabin, that's vandalizing it," Moreland said.

"That's one way to look at it, I guess," Cowles conceded. He was careful to maintain a friendly tone.

"Your place is down the river what, four or five miles?" Cowles asked. "I'll come down to see you one of these days."

"That's a good cabin you're going to burn down," Moreland said curtly. He turned and walked away.

Moreland stopped at the ranger station occasionally that fall, and Cowles told the cook to set another place at the table. Moreland said little during mealtime and didn't stay long after eating, when the crew sat on the porch talking, sometimes until stars dotted the blue-black, late-summer sky.

Cowles and Moreland had their first run-in when the ranger was told that someone was living in the Skull Creek Cabin. Cowles saddled his horse and rode up the river trail to check out the report. He was sure Moreland was the culprit, and he was apprehensive.

Moreland was sitting on the step in front of the cabin when Cowles rode up. Cowles did not dismount, but noticed that a fishing pole stood against the wall of the cabin.

"How's the fishing?" he asked.

"Pretty good," Moreland said. He pulled a fat rainbow trout out of each front pants pocket and held up the fish.

"Those are nice fish," Cowles said. "Have you been here long?"

"A couple of days."

"How did you get in?"

"I got caught in a rainstorm."

"Do you have a key, Bill?"

"It was raining pretty hard that night. We had lightning, too. What was that, two nights ago?"

"You can't stay, Bill," Cowles said. "It's against regulations."

"Maybe I could give you a few fish."

"We can't do that, Bill. You'll have to get your things and leave."

Moreland turned on his heel and disappeared into the cabin. Cowles waited for several moments. Finally, Moreland emerged with his packsack on his back and his rifle in his hands.

"I guess you won't be needing any fish," he said angrily. He brushed past Cowles' mount and headed down the trail. The little man was plainly irked; he did not stop at the ranger station again that fall.

That winter, Cowles hiked from Bungalow Ranger Station to Canyon with game warden Mel Francis on an annual mid-winter inspection tour of the forest. The second night out, the two men arrived at the Skull Creek Cabin, ravenous after a long day on the trail. The food in their packs was gone, but an ample supply of food was supposed to be stored at the cabin. The cabin, however, had been cleaned out. They were certain the Ridgerunner was to blame, and they spent an uncomfortable night because of their hunger.

The following March, Tom Kiiskila, a local back-country pilot, stopped Ralph Space on the sidewalk near the Forest Service office in Orofino.

"Who is stationed at Canyon?" Kiiskila asked. "I flew over the ranger station this morning and saw smoke coming from the chimney of one of the buildings. The snow was shoveled off the roofs, too."

"No one is at Canyon," Space said. "The ranger station is still closed for the winter."

That afternoon Space contacted the sheriff's office. The sheriff was unable to help, and Space told Cowles at a cocktail party that night that he would have to go to Canyon the next day and arrest the Ridgerunner. Cowles' evening was ruined.

The next morning, Cowles strapped on his .357 magnum pistol and flew into the forest with Kiiskila. Cowles had been deputized, and he carried a John Doe warrant for the arrest of whomever he found in the buildings at Canyon.

As Kiiskila and Cowles flew over Canyon, smoke curled up from one of the buildings, but the snow was too deep for Kiiskila to land, and he flew on to Cayuse Landing, an air field 60 miles from Canyon.

The state Fish & Game Department was using Cayuse Landing for an aerial game survey being conducted with helicopters. Cowles hoped to talk the pilot of one of the helicopters into flying him back to Canyon, but a driving snowstorm set in and Cowles and Kiiskila could not find the helicopters.

The next day, Kiiskila and Cowles spotted the helicopters at Kelly Forks Ranger Station 50 miles up the North Fork from Canyon. They landed despite a snowstorm, and Cowles convinced the pilot of one of the helicopters to fly him to Canyon.

The chopper set down at the ranger station at 10:45 a.m. The date was March 4, 1956.

Because of the noise from the helicopter, Moreland would know someone had arrived. Cowles wanted him to have time to think before their meeting. He walked around the grounds, checking the doors of the office, cookhouse, bunkhouse and warehouse. All were unlocked—and should not have been.

Smoke was still rising from the ranger's residence 25 minutes later when Cowles walked up to the door. He knocked and went in. Moreland was in the kitchen, mopping the floor. He was dressed in long johns, canvas pants and suspenders, but wore no shirt.

"Hello," Cowles said. He hoped his voice was calm.

"Hello," Moreland said. "I was just cleaning up. Would you like a cup of coffee?"

"Sure."

"I'll be done here in a minute." Moreland bent to his task, pushing the mop back and forth across the linoleum floor.

"Don't hurry," Cowles said. "Mind if I get the pilot? It's cold outside where he's waiting."

"Go ahead."

Cowles reached out the door and motioned with his arm. The pilot, "Swede" Nelson, stepped out of the bubble cockpit of his helicopter, walked across the yard and joined Cowles and Moreland in the building.

Moreland set three cups on the table and poured steaming coffee into them. The men sat down.

"Have you had a good winter?" Cowles asked.

"Yes," Moreland said. "I wish this contemptible snow would let up, though."

"Has the snow been hard on the game?"

"Yes, it has. A lot of elk have died this winter. Coyotes have been chasing the elk calves. I've put several of the dear varmints out of commission."

"Good," Cowles said.

"I also took care of some rats in the buildings."

"Oh. How did you do that?"

"I nailed a garbage can lid to a board to make a club. The can lid was so wide they couldn't get out of the way of it."

The three men sipped their coffee.

"How was your winter?" Moreland asked.

"Fine," Cowles replied.

"How long have you been here?"

"About a week. I've been here two or three times this winter for about a week each time. This is a nice place. Is it yours?"

"It's the government's, of course, but I'm supposed to stay here when I come out from Orofino."

"If I were you, I'd stay here all the time."

Cowles had not yet lived in the new ranger's residence, which had been built the previous fall. Moreland had beaten him to it; he was the first occupant of the building, in fact, and he had not kept the place clean.

From where Cowles sat, he could see into the bedroom. Rumpled clothes lay on the floor, and a pair of Moreland's sox decorated the back of a chair.

In the kitchen, dirty dishes sat everywhere among empty, half-full, and unopened cans of food. Cowles knew that no food had been stored in the building the previous fall. The food must have come from the cookhouse.

Moreland had been cooking in the living room on the heating stove, which wasn't meant for that purpose. Smoke had darkened the walls and ceiling of the room, though its paint was still new. Moreland apparently had not opened the damper when he used the stove. Cowles expected that the few minutes of mopping he had seen Moreland do was the only cleaning the building had received all winter.

Moreland told Cowles he had been feeding racoons inside the building. He showed Cowles chunks of meat he carried in his pants pockets to give the creatures. The meat was wrapped in shreds of wax paper.

"I've been keeping the snow shoveled off the roofs," Moreland said. "I've done a few other things, too. A porcupine was getting under the warehouse and chewing on the floor joists, but I put some screens over the holes where the dear little thing was getting in."

"Good," Cowles said.

Again the three men sipped their coffee in silence. It was only a matter of time before Cowles had to tell Moreland he was taking him in. Cowles tried to broach the subject as gently as possible.

"How did you get in?" he asked matter-of-factly.

"I have a key," Moreland said.

"Where did you get it?"

"Stratton gave it to me when he was the ranger. You knew Stratton, didn't you?"

"I've heard about him. From what I've heard, he was a nice fellow."

"Yes, he was. He gave me the key because I'm a special agent of the government."

Cowles knew that no ranger in his right mind would give Moreland a key.

"Bill," Cowles said, "I'm going to have to arrest you for being in the buildings. I've got a warrant here."

Cowles pulled the warrant from his jacket pocket and held it out. Moreland ignored the piece of paper.

"Don't arrest me now," he said. "I've got all my gold down at Milk Creek."

"I'm sorry, Bill," Cowles said, "but I've got to take you in. No one will bother your gold."

"Well, I'm not going," Moreland responded, his voice rising.

"I'm not leaving without you, Bill," Cowles persisted. "I don't want any trouble, but I've got orders to carry out."

The pilot interrupted. "Have you ever been in a helicopter, Bill?" he asked. "That's a pretty nice bird out there. It flies low and can hover over a herd of elk. You get a good view of the mountains and the game. I'll take you up to Kelly Creek where there's a plane waiting."

"No, I guess I haven't been in a chopper," Moreland said. His voice softened. He seemed intrigued by the idea of a helicopter ride.

"Where's the key Stratton gave you?" Cowles asked.

"I don't have the key with me," Moreland replied. "It's down at my cabin. I opened the buildings so I could get some work done, then took my key back down to Milk Creek. I don't like to carry a government key around."

"We can land the chopper at your cabin and get the key," Cowles offered.

"Oh, no, there's too much snow at Milk Creek to land the chopper."

"All right, we'll forget about the key," Cowles said. He would not force Moreland to look for a key they both knew was hidden elsewhere.

Cowles gave Moreland a receipt for his rifle and pistol and left the guns at the ranger station. Moreland enjoyed the helicopter ride, but Cowles did not. Moreland sat between Cowles and the pilot, and Cowles had a recurring thought as he looked out the open side of the doorless bubble cockpit. "What would happen if he pulled my seat belt open and gave me a shove?" Cowles wondered. After the helicopter landed at Kelly Creek, Kiiskila flew Cowles and Moreland on to Orofino.

That night, Cowles read four letters he had confiscated from Moreland at the ranger station. The letters were fascinating. They indicated that Moreland was tired of winter but utterly taken with the wildlife around the ranger station.

"Obscured from all earthly creatures and screaming with unsurpressed delight each time he glances at his elementary control room the Great Elementary Director spent almost twenty-eight days amusing himself by way of creating misery for earthy humans," Moreland wrote. "One would almost think that he had created a switch that worked alternately from rain to snow. There could also be a possibility that the switch that controls the sun was jarred loose by an atom bomb test. Personally I believe he is just testing to see what people can survive under."

Cowles knew the winters at Canyon were long, but he had never heard them ascribed to such causes. He was also impressed by Moreland's vocabulary.

Moreland went on to claim that he had fed the elk hay from the barn at Canyon, and the animals grew to trust him so much they let him pet them. The idea that someone could pet elk struck Cowles as far-fetched. The wapiti, the species of elk that roamed the Clearwater Mountains, were extremely shy animals. Still, with hay to attract them when they had little food, and with plenty of time on his hands to gain their trust, perhaps Moreland did pet them. Cowles imagined what a sight that would be.

The second of Moreland's letters was nearly a word-for-word duplication of the first, and like the first letter it included an account of an experience with a family of raccoons.

"This family consisted of two winsome youngsters and what seemed to be the parents," Moreland wrote. "I experienced a few bad thoughts about crime as I stood there watching them eat some of my coyote bait. What would J. Edgar Hoover do should news reach his excellency's office that a bald kidnapping had been engineered in the shadow of a government station, as their home is close by the cookshack? I certainly think carrying one of them home with me would be a criminal act."

The second letter, undated like the first, included a joyous note about a hint of spring.

"This evening I watched the thick mass of white fog as it slowly disappeared revealing those beautiful and almost inaccessible green mountains surrounding the Canyon Ranger Station," Moreland wrote.

"About 30 minutes of that hot sun bearing almost straight down at me where I am shoveling snow erased every vestige of doubt from my mind that spring was not rapidly approaching."

The third and fourth letters, sent to Forest Service offices in Orofino and Missoula, proposed building a dam on a creek uphill from the ranger station to generate hydroelectric power.

"This small plant would or could be used for educational purposes there," one of the letters said. It added, "To date I have put 13 coyotes and four bobcats out of commission this past winter."

Moreland also said that he had raised the flag on Christmas Day.

Cowles filed the letters. He thought they might be useful as evidence, but he was wrong.

Moreland was in jail for 60 days, but no charges were filed. The prosecuting attorney said the matter was a federal case and declined to bring state charges. U.S. Attorney Sherman F. Furey Jr. decided against filing federal charges, and Moreland was set free.

Ralph Space was furious. What more could he do to get Moreland out of his hair? Moreland had been caught red-handed in a violation of law, then was let go without court action of any kind. Space wrote Forest Service attorney Morris Hankins seeking action.

"We are at something of a loss in deciding what we should do in this case," he said. Space told Hankins that the district judge and prosecuting attorney thought Moreland did little harm and that his depredations should be prosecuted in federal court.

"Locally, the people are rather amused by the difficulties Mr. Moreland causes the Forest Service," Space said. "To them, it is something of a game and they get a kick out of seeing Moreland escape punishment for offenses that do not directly concern them."

Furey, the U.S. attorney, answered Space through Hankins, noting, "... it has not been very long since it was considered entirely proper for a traveler to take shelter in a stranger's cabin and use whatever facilities therein which were necessary to sustain him. It was indicated, also, that Moreland had shoveled snow off the roofs of all the buildings, which would indicate a neighborly, rather than a criminal or malicious attitude toward the owner of the buildings."

Furey's reply did not mollify Space. The buildings at Canyon had peaked roofs that shed snow even when they weren't shoveled; Space thought Moreland had done the government no service.

A month after Moreland was set free, he sent a bill to Space at the supervisor's office. He claimed that he had cleared brush from a trail, and the Forest Service owed him $12 for his labor. Space rejected the claim in an angry letter.

"No payment will be made for any work you may have performed or any that you will perform in the future," Space wrote. "It is noticed that you have taken the title of 'acting ranger.' This you have done without authority from the Forest Service, and you are warned to stop such practice at once."

Moreland ignored Space's letter. He continued to refer to his cabin as the Milk Creek Sub-station—and to himself as the acting ranger.

*F*OURTEEN

When Floyd Cowles closed Canyon Ranger Station after the 1956 work season, he wrote a memorandum warning the Ridgerunner to stay out of the buildings. Cowles tacked the memorandum to the dry provisions cabinet in the station office, where he was sure Moreland would see it. The note was gone when crewmen John DeBarber and John Williams arrived in January.

Several items that DeBarber and Williams had left at Canyon the previous fall also were missing, including DeBarber's .45-caliber Colt automatic pistol, several boxes of ammunition, a hunting knife, and a poncho. A pair of Forest Service snowshoes also had been taken.

Cowles had put a combination lock on the door of the root cellar, which was near the station office. The lock was gone, and a file lay in front of the door amid a pile of steel shavings.

DeBarber and Williams, who were to stay at Canyon for several weeks, saw Moreland a few days after they arrived. He came out of the timber, walking through the snow into the yard, where they were peeling bark from fresh-cut poles. He wore the missing pair of snowshoes, having blotted out the Forest Service insignia on them with pitch.

"Where's the 'thing' that runs the place?" he demanded.

"If you mean the ranger, he hasn't been here lately," DeBarber said.

"I saw that big Space pet and another fellow walk across the bridge and up the river toward Canyon a few weeks ago," Moreland said.

"He was here a while back," said DeBarber, guessing that Moreland saw Cowles before the ranger left for the winter.

"He broke the upstairs window from the inside," Moreland said. "There was glass out in the yard. Why did he come out here?"

"I don't know," Williams said. He and DeBarber were certain that Cowles had broken no windows.

"Someone killed an elk down the river last fall," Moreland said. "They left a Forest Service camera hanging from a branch. I've got the camera down at Milk Creek if you want it."

"Okay," Williams said.

"Are you going to be staying for a while?" Moreland asked.

"Yes."

"I've got to go. I've got lots of miles to cover today."

Moreland headed back into the forest. DeBarber and Williams didn't see him again for two weeks, and when he showed up he was armed. The two Forest Service men offered Moreland a cup of coffee, and he accepted. The three men went inside the ranger's office.

"Where are you headed?" DeBarber asked.

"I'm going up the trail to the Bungalow and then out to town."

"Do you think you'll make it to Flat Creek tonight?" DeBarber said. It was the middle of the afternoon, and Flat Creek was 13 miles farther.

"I doubt it," Moreland said. The little man was quiet. His rifle laid across his knees while he sipped his coffee. He said little more and left within a half hour.

DeBarber and Williams hiked to the Skull Creek Cabin the next day and found fuel in the bottom of a coffee can used for filling lanterns. The food supplies had been tapped, and several chunks of firewood had been burned. Moreland apparently had used the cabin.

The two crewmen returned to town in late March. The ranger station was opened for the season on May 9, 1957, and by then Cowles had transferred and been replaced by Ted Hay.

Hay found nothing out of place when he opened the station, but a McCulloch chain saw was missing from the Skull Creek Cabin. He contacted the FBI, and agents Ed Mayer and Stein Gourd flew into the forest. They went to Moreland's cabin; he told them he had the missing chain saw and DeBarber's .45-caliber pistol.

The agents did not arrest Moreland, but before they left they disassembled his rifle. If he wanted to take a shot at them, he would have to reassemble the gun, and their helicopter would be out of range by the time he had the gun back together. The agents took DeBarber's pistol with them.

The pistol's serial number had been filed off, but the FBI crime lab in Washington, D.C., was able to decipher it. It matched a number that DeBarber had given the agents. Identifying the pistol was important, Mayer believed. He thought the FBI couldn't make a case against Moreland solely on his possession of a Forest Service chain saw. Equipment was sometimes left behind on the fire line, and Moreland might claim he found the saw at a fire site.

Gourd and Mayer flew back into the forest on Oct. 31 to arrest Moreland. Mayer directed the pilot to set his helicopter down a mile from the mouth of Milk Creek so Moreland could not take a shot at the machine.

As the helicopter flew past Moreland's place out over the river, the agents heard shots. Mayer suspected Moreland was firing into the ground or across the river to intimidate him and Gourd. Mayer still doubted that Moreland would hurt anyone.

As soon as the helicopter set down, Mayer and Gourd set off for Moreland's cabin. They heard no more shots.

Hay, who had walked down the river from Canyon, was hidden in the brush near Moreland's place when Mayer and Gourd arrived. He stepped out of the brush to greet the FBI agents; the three men talked in hushed tones.

"I heard gunfire when you flew past Moreland's place," Hay said.

"Did you see whether he was shooting at us?" Mayer asked.

"No. I was too far upriver to see where he was aiming."

"I think he was just trying to scare us, but be on your guard," Mayer said.

The three men went to the door. Moreland answered their knock. He was wearing a Forest Service hard hat with the words "Special Agent in Charge, Milk Creek Sub-Station" scrawled across the crown on a piece of tape.

Moreland invited his visitors inside and directed them to sit on wooden fruit boxes that served as chairs. The cabin was filled with junk. Moreland had been cooking on a washtub turned upside down, and the building smelled heavily of smoke. Food cans and boxes crammed the shelves, taking up every available square inch of space. Grease spots covered the paper label on a big can of Edwards coffee that sat on the shelf. A raccoon worked around the legs of Moreland's table and along the front of his counter, looking for tidbits.

"Just a minute," Moreland said. "I've got to feed this fellow."

He pulled a gob of wax paper from his pocket and unwrapped it. There were small bits of putrid meat inside, and he fed some of the meat to the raccoon. The animal had known what to expect as soon as Moreland reached in his pocket, and it stood on its hind legs and accepted the meat from Moreland's hand. It seemed tame, and when Moreland sat down it jumped onto his lap.

"He's been with me all winter," Moreland said proudly.

"Bill, we're going to have to take you back with us," Mayer said. "I'm sorry you will have to leave your friend, but you're under arrest."

"What I ought to do is disarm all of you and hold the ship," Moreland said. "I could do it, too."

"Bill, you would never live to complete the job," Mayer said.

Hay asked Moreland whether he had been in the buildings at Canyon during the winter.

"Hell, yes," Moreland snapped. "Every time I go by I go in. I guess I've been in there 900 times or more."

Despite his outburst, Moreland went peacefully with the FBI agents. He talked animatedly as the helicopter flew out of the mountains. He knew the name of each peak, and he took pride in his knowledge of the country.

"I've been over that ridge in the winter," he said, pointing at the craggy outcroppings of a particularly rough mountain. "That's Goat Ridge. There's a lot of snow up there in the winter. A fellow doesn't run into many people on Goat Ridge then."

Three streams plunged down the sheer, rocky face of Goat Ridge like tears running down the roughened cheeks of an old person. Mayer stared at the mountain. It was beautiful—and inhospitable.

As the helicopter flew along, Moreland told Mayer of other spots where he had been and pointed them out, speaking as though his travels were of great importance. Mayer marveled at the country's vastness and emptiness. Most people, Mayer thought, would have had been overcome by the isolation and loneliness if they had lived as Moreland had lived.

"The hardest times were when it was raining," Moreland said. "You'd get wet clear through and couldn't dry out. That was miserable."

The helicopter flew Mayer and Moreland to Boehl's Cabin, where Moreland had worked years before. After the pilot landed, he took Mayer aside and told him that Moreland had named each mountain peak correctly.

The FBI agent and his prisoner were driven across back roads to St. Maries and on to Lewiston, where Moreland was arraigned late in the afternoon before U.S. Magistrate Earl Christy. The Ridgerunner, still wearing his safety helmet, stood beside his packsack in the courtroom as he faced the judge.

"What is your occupation?" Christy asked.

"I don't suppose I have any," Moreland replied.

"Mr. Moreland, you are charged with the theft of a power saw from the Skull Creek Cabin, an installation of the United States Government. You have the right..."

"The Forest Service doesn't keep a power saw at the Skull Creek Cabin," Moreland interjected.

"What, Mr. Moreland?"

"They don't keep a power saw at Skull Creek. They keep one in the warehouse at Canyon."

"Mr. Moreland, you are interrupting this court."

"There's no reason to keep a power saw at Skull Creek. They keep a crosscut saw there."

"That's immaterial," Christy said. "Mr. Moreland, you have the right to a preliminary hearing to establish whether a crime has been committed and whether probable cause exists to believe that you committed that crime. Do you want a preliminary hearing?"

"No. Lock me up."

"Very well. This case is continued until Nov. 13, at which time you will enter a plea to the charge. Bail is set at $1,000. Do you wish to post bail?"

"I don't have any money."

"The prisoner is remanded to the custody of the sheriff in lieu of bail."

Moreland was taken to Coeur d'Alene and jailed. He entered a plea of not guilty two weeks later and was sent to Orofino for psychiatric evaluation at the State Hospital North. A sanity hearing was to follow the evaluation.

At a few minutes before 10 on the morning of Jan. 8, 1958, Deputy U.S. Marshal J. Bruce Blake went to the Clearwater County Jail to escort Moreland to his sanity hearing.

"I need the Ridgerunner," the six-foot, six-inch Blake told the deputy on duty.

A few minutes later Moreland was led out of the cell block and into the anteroom of the jail.

"Hello, Bill," said Blake, who had driven Moreland between jails in the past. "We've got a few minutes before we have to be in court. Would you like a smoke?"

"Sure," Moreland said. The two men sat down on a bench in the hallway outside the sheriff's office.

"How are things in jail?" Blake asked.

"I miss my animals," Moreland said. "I had a raccoon that was living with me when they brought me in."

"Did you have any other critters?"

"I had a pet mouse all last winter. He used to sleep with me, but I rolled over on him one night and killed him."

"What about your shack? Do you miss it?"

"I wish I was still there. I drew down on those contemptible pets in the helicopter when they were on their way in. I could have shot them out of the air. I considered it. They were sitting ducks. I could have picked them off, or the operator."

"You'd just be in a heap more trouble than you are now."

A psychiatrist from the State Hospital North attended Moreland's sanity hearing, but did not testify. He sat at one of the tables provided for counsel, and as the proceedings got under way, he put snuff into his nostrils. Blake turned to Mayer and said, "We've got the wrong S.O.B. up for examinatiom here, Eddie."

The psychiatrist did not testify. Ralph Space, who had never met Moreland, was the only witness. He said in an affidavit that Moreland was "mentally deficient" and "of such low intelligence that he cannot properly handle his business and personal affairs and has been and can be exploited." Judge Ben Bear found that Moreland was insane and ordered him committed to the State Hospital North at Orofino.

As Blake led Moreland away from the courtroom, the little man said, "I don't want to go to the hospital with the sheriff. I don't trust him. I'll go with you."

Blake agreed to transport Moreland to the asylum, but was unfamiliar with the institution and was unsure where to take his prisoner. As they drove around the grounds, Moreland said, "Drop me off at that building there."

A sign said that the structure was the Administration Building; Blake slowed his car to turn into the parking area.

"No, go around to the back," Moreland said. "I've been here before, you know."

As Blake pulled to a stop at the rear of the building, Moreland let himself out of the car and disappeared through the double glass doors. Blake put his car in reverse, backed out of the parking area and headed for town.

Moreland accepted institution life. He lived in an open ward, which meant that he could come and go as he pleased as long as he didn't leave the hospital grounds. At night the ward was locked.

He was fond of dancing and playing cards and got along with the other inmates and the staff. He worked in the hospital laundry, where he sorted donated clothing. Inmates cleaned and mended the useful items, which were sold to raise money for the hospital.

Moreland also tended the flower beds on the grounds and worked in the huge hospital garden, which was on a hillside near the Clearwater River. He was good at gardening, and staff members commented on his work. They saw little of the moodiness that had plagued Moreland in the past.

On April 10, 1959, Moreland walked away from the hospital. A few days later, a helicopter pilot saw smoke coming from the hovel at Milk Creek. The pilot, who knew Moreland, landed and asked the little man if he would like a ride back to the hospital. Moreland said that he would, and his return caused a sensation when the helicopter set down on the hospital's expansive green lawn.

Early in the morning of Aug. 2, 1963, Moreland wriggled through a small window in his ward and fled from the institution. This time he wasn't going back. A log truck driver picked him up on the highway later that day and gave him a ride to Pierce; late that afternoon a Cat skinner saw him walking down the road to Canyon miles from Pierce.

The next morning a logger who was living with his family in a small trailer in the woods awakened to find that his son's raft had been taken to the opposite side of the river. It was assumed Moreland had used the raft.

Later that day, a Forest Service employee met Moreland on the trail that ran along the North Fork. He talked with Moreland, who introduced himself as Bill Smith.

"I thought your name was Moreland," the Forest Service worker said.

"I don't use that name any more," Moreland said. "Too much trouble has been associated with that name."

"Where are you headed?"

"I came back to see if these mountains were as beautiful as I remembered them or if I had just imagined it all. I'm not going to stay."

Other reports filtered in that Moreland had talked with a lookout on Wallow Mountain and a logger who worked at Big Island, which was on the North Fork downriver from Canyon.

One night in December, four months after Moreland had fled from the hospital, loud coughing awakened Betty Bailey, the cook at Canyon Ranger Station. The coughing came from a mobile home that was next door to Mrs. Bailey's trailer in the housing area of the ranger station. A man named Art Riley lived next to Mrs. Bailey, and as the rasping continued, she assumed that Riley was ill.

After a poor night's sleep, Mrs. Bailey went to the cookhouse at 5 a.m. to start breakfast. She had set out three slabs of bacon, four loaves of bread, and a sack of pancake mix the night before, but the items were gone.

Mrs. Bailey was stunned. She went outside. It was still dark, but a skiff of snow covered the ground, and she could see a set of footprints in the moonlight. The footprints led away from the cookhouse. Whoever made them had come from Riley's trailer. Then Mrs. Bailey remembered. Riley was gone. She had heard someone else coughing in his trailer.

Mrs. Bailey shivered, glanced around, and went back into the cookhouse. She put coffee on for the crew, then paused to think for a moment. She had heard all about the Ridgerunner, and she was certain that he must have taken the food. She decided, however, that she would tell no one. The Ridgerunner might be a problem for her bosses, but she felt sorry for the man. She believed he had been harassed by the Forest Service; she was certain he needed the food more than the government did.

Canyon was to be closed for the winter that day. Mrs. Bailey had just enough time to get another sack of pancake flour from the winter stores before the flunky arrived to help with breakfast. She retrieved the flour quickly and kept quiet about the missing items.

The last person to see Moreland in the Clearwater country was a logger named Jake Altmiller. Altmiller had known Moreland for years. When the little man lived at Milk Creek, Altmiller usually had been his first visitor in the spring.

Altmiller was anxious to buck the rapids when spring arrived; he made a point of being the first boatman up the North Fork after the ice broke up. He brought Moreland tobacco on his visits, and the little man was glad to have something to put in his pipe.

Altmiller once took a boatload of relatives to Moreland's shack on the 4th of July. It was the only time he took women to the place, and Moreland was delighted to have female visitors. He talked for a long time about his garden and was especially proud of his strawberries. "It's just a race between me and the ground squirrels and the robins whenever a berry turns red," he said. Despite his good humor, Moreland gave Altmiller's wife the feeling that he was looking right through her with his sharp eyes.

Sometimes Moreland was in no mood to receive company. On one trip up the river, Altmiller didn't bother to stop. He saw Moreland hidden in the brush with a .300 Savage rifle across his knees. Moreland was gnashing his teeth and obviously distraught; afterwards, Altmiller made it a point not to turn in to shore unless Moreland came out to greet him.

Altmiller learned how far Moreland's reputation had spread when he hauled a U.S. Coast & Geodetic Survey crew from California up the North Fork. As Altmiller's boat approached Milk Creek, one of the USGS scientists grew nervous.

"That's the Ridgerunner's place up there," said the man. "When you go by, stay on the opposite side of the river."

While Moreland was at State Hospital North, Altmiller picked greens from his untended garden. Altmiller suspected that Moreland returned to his hovel after fleeing from the hospital, but he did not see Moreland at Milk Creek through the fall of 1963.

The next spring, Altmiller sawed logs on a landing on the road to Canyon, which had been widened and converted to two lanes. Altmiller cut the logs into uniform lengths so they could be loaded onto logging trucks. The landing was a wide, flat area where logs were stacked and the big trucks had plenty of room to turn around.

Altmiller was sawing away at 9 a.m. one morning when he saw Moreland walking along the road. The little man carried a packsack on his back and was hiking purposefully toward Pierce. Altmiller shut off his saw.

"Bill, wait a minute," he called.

"Hello, Jake," Moreland said as Altmiller came up. He took his pack off his back and set it on the ground. The two shook hands.

"Did you spend the winter in the mountains?" Altmiller asked.

"Yes, I did," Moreland said.

"Where are you going?"

"I'm leaving."

"I thought these mountains were your home, Bill."

"They were, but there are too many people here for me now."

Altmiller studied Moreland's face. The little man's whiskers were grayer than he remembered, but Moreland's eyes still flashed with the same old intensity.

"Should I keep an eye on your cabin, or are you leaving for good?" Altmiller asked.

"I'm leaving for good," Moreland said.

"Well, good luck to you," Altmiller said.

"Same to you."

The two men shook hands again, and the Ridgerunner lifted his pack onto his shoulders and walked away. Altmiller watched until he disappeared from view behind a curve in the road.

That fall, giant cedars came crashing to earth as the Forest Service opened the Isabella Creek drainage to logging; not long thereafter, timber cutting began in the Skull Creek drainage.

Epilogue

The North Fork changed drastically after the Ridgerunner left. In 1973, the U.S. Army Corps of Engineers finished filling the reservoir behind Dworshak Dam, which was built near the mouth of the river. The 700-foot tall dam, the third highest in the world when it was built, backed water for 53 miles. Boaters and water skiers plied the huge reservoir, and the state planted kokanee, a landlocked salmon. The dam ended the spawning runs of Chinook salmon and steelhead, the latter of which was the world's largest strain.

The dam chased Perd Hughes and other North Fork residents out of the river canyon. Hughes, who was in his 60s, became ill and died a few years later. The water inundated his ingenious lodge and Moreland's hovel at Milk Creek. It ended its advance four miles from Canyon.

Jake Altmiller pulled out, too. He bought a place east of Orofino, but missed the river. It had been a liquid highway to his favorite haunts. He thought often of his spring trips up the river, when he saw deer and elk by the thousands along the banks, waiting for the snow to melt so they could migrate back to the high country.

The Forest Service tore down the Bungalow Ranger Station and downgraded the Canyon station to a work center. The Canyon ranger was moved to the forest supervisor's office in Orofino, 60 miles from the Canyon district.

Most of the lookout towers fell into disuse as the Forest Service turned to airplanes with infrared heat sensors for fire patrol. In the new Forest Service, fire crews might come by aircraft and bus from hundreds of miles away, and their ranks would include women.

The new road to Canyon was paved to the ranger station and punched on through to the old site of the Bungalow, opening up 26 miles of river that had never seen motor vehicles. Campgrounds were built along the new road, and other roads snaked their way into the hills to the Ridgerunner's haunts. Some of the trails became so overgrown that hikers had trouble finding them.

The roads allowed tourists to reach many new points in the spectacular mountains, but they changed the country. Debates still rage over how much more land should be opened up. The effect that logging would have on the elk is at issue, but no one claims the Forest Service is poisoning the elk. The man who leveled that charge left long ago.

People still talk about the Ridgerunner. Orval Chase, a long-time Clearwater County resident, enjoys telling how the Ridgerunner asked him for a job in the '50s.

Chase, a tall pleasant man who years ago did everything from farming to spearing steelhead to make a living, was standing near the green chain at the Cardiff Mill when Moreland walked up.

"You're the boss, I guess," Moreland began.

"That's right," Chase replied.

"I'm looking for a job. I'm known around here as the Ridgerunner. I've got kind of a poor reputation, but I didn't blow up that Cat over at the Potlatch even though they laid that on me."

"I don't have anything right now," Chase said.

"I might be back around again."

Louis Turcotte told Chase that he arrived at his cabin on Orogrande Creek near Bungalow Ranger Station to find the Ridgerunner emerging from the door.

"Who gave you permission to be here?" Turcotte asked.

"Well, I didn't really have permission, but the roof was going to break down if I didn't shovel the snow," Moreland answered. "I also used a little piece of bacon you had in there."

Turcotte eyed the roof. He couldn't see that a single shovelful of snow had been removed. He was an easygoing man, however, and he liked Moreland instantly. He allowed Moreland to spend the night. When

Moreland prepared to leave the next day, Turcotte pulled two snow shovels from under the building and asked Moreland to help him shovel the roof. Moreland readily agreed. He visited Turcotte often after that.

Moreland dropped in and out of people's lives, and sometimes they didn't realize it. Bud Ripley discussed the weather and lumber prices with a friendly middle-aged man at the lunch counter in a Pierce hotel at noon one day. When the man left, Ripley asked the waiter who he was. "That's the Ridgerunner," the waiter replied.

Moton Roark saw Moreland on a Lewiston street peering into a store window at Christmastime. Roark lowered his shoulder and playfully bumped into Moreland. The two shook hands and talked for a long time.

Nobody seems to know what became of Moreland. The state of Idaho has no record of his death, nor does the state of Kentucky, where he was born. Bert Curtis, an old adversary, thought Moreland died in the mountains "and the coyotes or a bobcat cleaned up the bones." Curtis himself died in 1985.

Jake Altmiller knew most of the people in the Clearwater country who were acquainted with Moreland. He has heard nothing of the man. Red McCollister, who hauled Moreland out of the woods to meet with Howard Bradbury, believes Moreland would be seen if he were still in the woods. Since Moreland was born in 1900, it's unlikely that he could have followed his nomadic lifestyle for many more years.

Still, four million acres in the middle of Idaho have been set aside as wilderness, and many other places in the west, in Canada, and in Alaska could give him the two things he craved: wild land and solitude.

He was an expert at living in such places, and recluses still turn up from time to time. A few years ago, a Montana resident came upon an improbably old man who claimed he lived in the Mission Mountains year-round. If such a man can endure, perhaps the Ridgerunner is out there still, ignoring the laws of man, tempting the forces of nature, and cheating the odds.

After his capture, Moreland sometimes visited crew members at Canyon Ranger Station, carrying unwrapped fish and huckleberries in the same packsack back to his cabin after trips up the river.

photo: Homer Stratton

The office at Canyon Ranger Station on the North Fork of the Clearwater River.

Moreland raising the flag in front of his shelter at Milk Creek.
photos: Louie Jacobsen

Canyon Ranger Floyd Cowles and the Ridgerunner at Canyon on March 4, 1956, the day Cowles arrested the Ridgerunner and took him out of the woods.

Moton Roark, who tracked down the Ridgerunner, was an adept woodsman.

Ranger Leroy Lewis, (shown here in 1921) feared the Ridgerunner might harm a crew member or dependent.

Bud Ripley in 1942. He shared a tent camp the Ridgerunner entered that year as he made the first of his thefts.

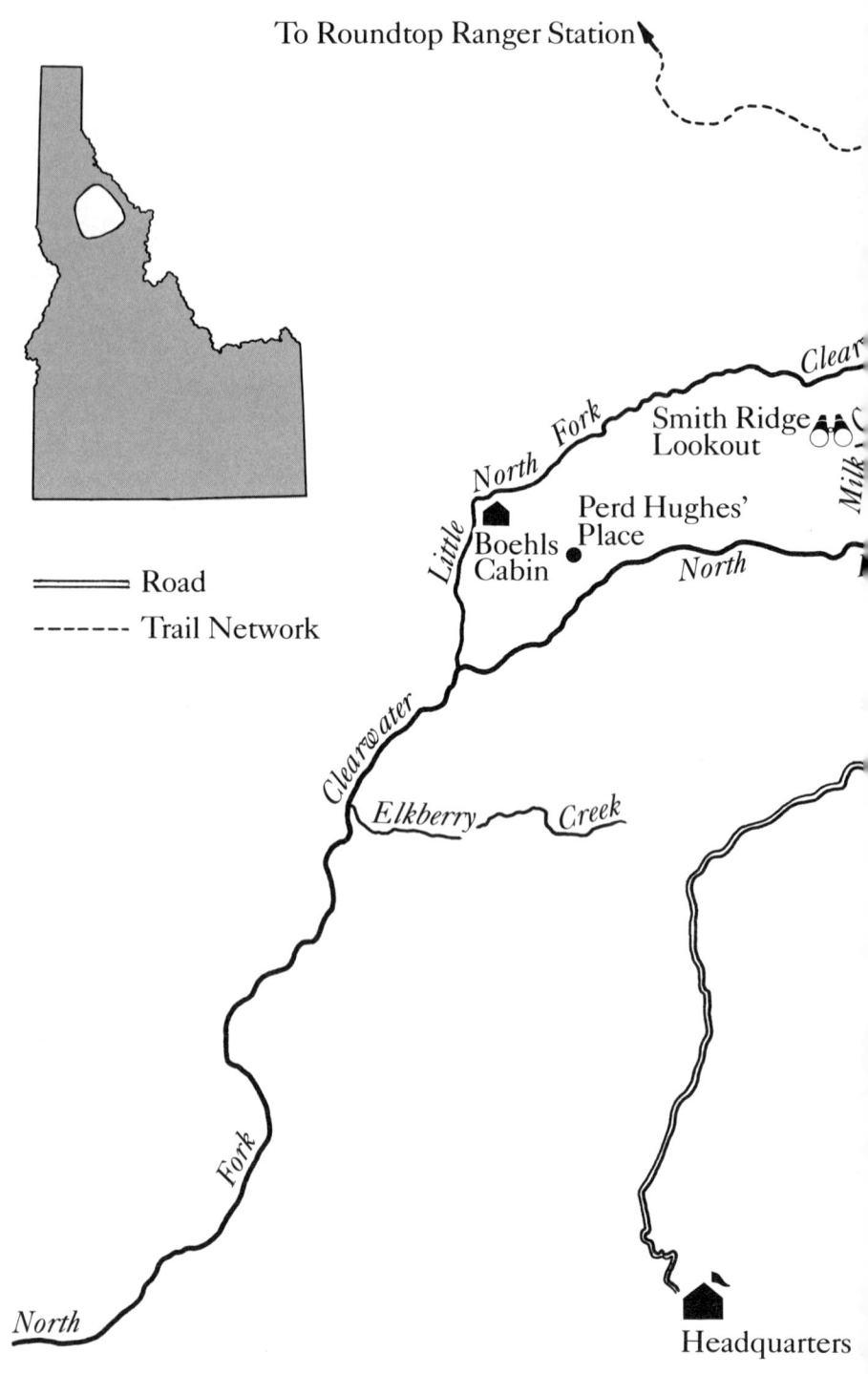

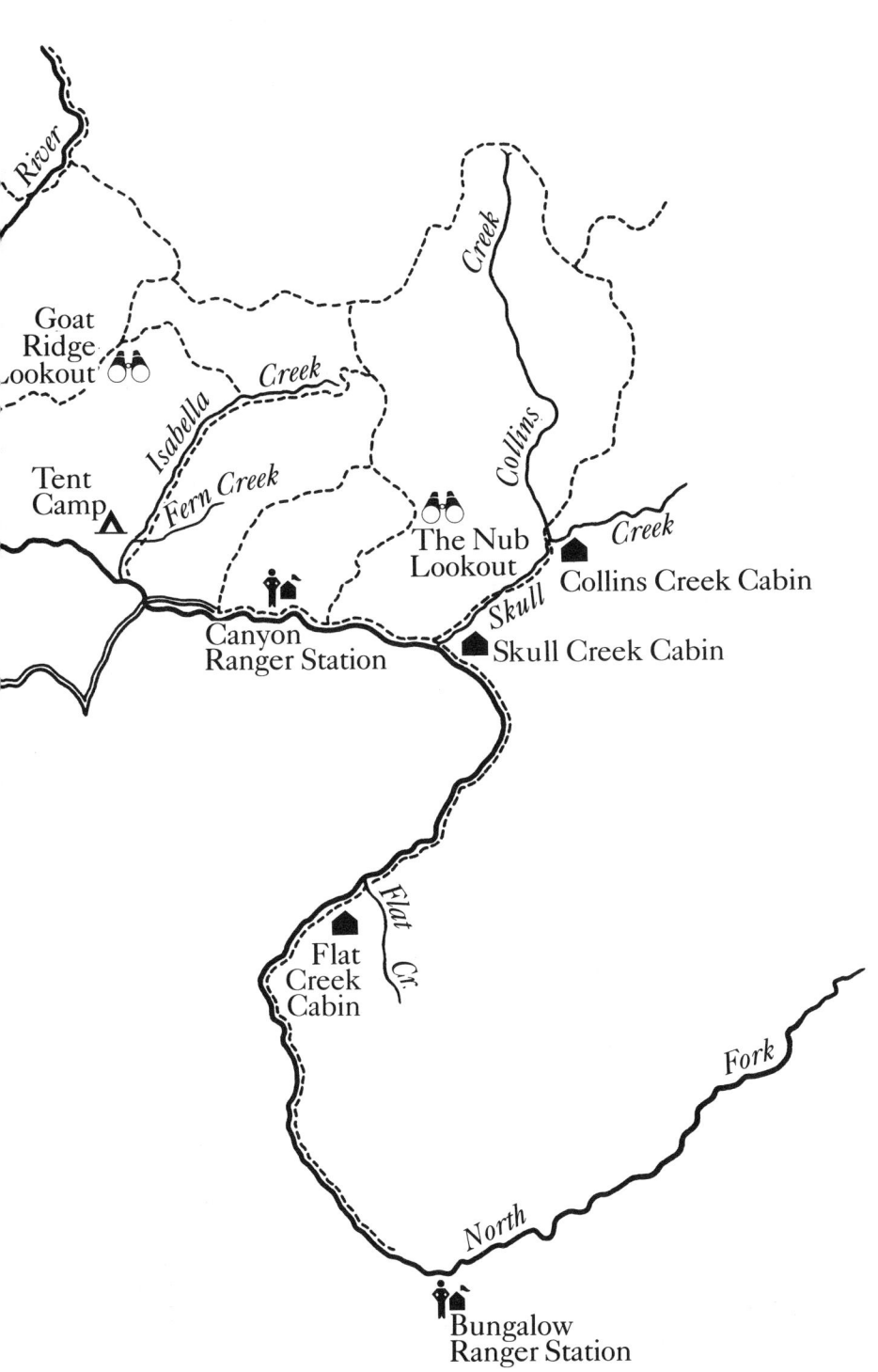

INDEX

Alder Creek Blister Rust Camp   11
Altmiller, Jake   148, 149, 151, 153
Amsbaugh, Byron   49, 57, 58, 60, 63, 66, 68, 69
Arizona State Prison at Florence   60, 82
Arkansas State Prison, Tupper Farm   60
Asotin, Washington   83
Atlanta   72
Avery   4, 7, 25, 26, 31, 72
Avery Ranger Station   4, 7, 9

Barry, Ed   42, 47
Bathtub Mountain   5, 25
Bear, Probate Judge Ben   146
Bear Skull Mountain   25, 77
Beardmore, George   100-102, 106, 108
Beaver Creek Flume   68
Bernard Cabin   74, 75

Bertha Hill Lookout   23
Big Island   99, 147
Bingo Saddle   101
Bitterroot Mountains   62, 115
Bitterroot Divide   4
Black Mountain   75
Blake, Deputy U.S. Marshal J. Bruce   145, 146
Boehl's Cabin   78, 87-89, 91, 144
Boise   8
Boll, Wallace   112
Boston Mountain   65
Bradbury, Howard   91, 92, 95-101, 103, 105, 110-112, 121, 153
Bradbury, Marjorie   95, 105
Bringman, Frank   121
Brown, Bill   3-9, 11
Bungalow Ranger Station   14, 32, 34, 35, 43, 121, 122, 134, 142, 151, 152
Buzzard Roost   8, 9
Buzzard, William   2, 9

Calder   31
Camp 6,   pg. 69
Camp 14,   pg. 40, 47, 69, 90, 101
Camp 42,   pg. 90
Camp 60,   pg. 91, 101, 123
Camp P   62
Camp T   62, 78, 90-93, 95, 96, 98-101, 105, 106, 110
Camp T Flume   92, 101, 112
Camp W   65
Camp X   85, 86, 103
Canyon Ranger District   14, 42, 43, 73, 75, 123
Canyon Ranger Station   9, 11, 13, 14, 23, 30, 32, 40, 58, 76, 79, 85, 99, 100, 124, 138, 141, 151, 152
Cardiff Mill   152
Carver, U.S. District Attorney John   81
Cayuse Creek   74
Cedars Ranger Station, The   74, 75
Chamberlain Basin   73, 82
Chase, Orval   152
Chateau Rock   121
Christy, U.S. Magistrate Earl   144, 145
Clearwater Mountains   8, 42, 73, 138
Clearwater National Forest   1, 12, 26, 32, 42
Clearwater River   12, 23, 147
Clearwater Timber Co.   90
Clearwater Timber Protective Association (CTPA)   86, 87, 89, 100, 122, 123
Clearwater Tribune, The   70
Clukey, "Silent Joe"   125, 127, 131
Cold Springs   77
Cole, Clyde   33-36, 41, 42, 78
Collins Creek   22, 24, 38

Collins Creek Cabin   23, 31, 36, 41, 46, 48, 65, 76, 77, 79
Conard, Sheriff Jack   35, 43, 70
Covington, Kentucky   71
Cowles, Ranger Floyd   132-139, 141, 142
Cox, Del   122
Cramer, A.J. "Bert"   8, 31, 70, 75-77, 79-81
Curtis, Bert   123, 130, 131, 153

Davis, Frank   40, 61, 79
DeBarber, John   141-143
Deep Creek Ranger Station   64, 73, 74
Dennis, John   25
Dent   14
Dial, Melvin   75
Dixie   73
Durant, Mickey   35-41, 44, 45, 48, 61
Dworshack Dam   151

Eagle Point   22, 64
Eagle City   9
Earp, Wyatt   9
Edelblute, Bernajean   95, 107
Edelblute, Lawrence "Boots"   95, 100, 101, 105-107
Elbow Bend Ranger Station   64
Elizabeth Creek   15
Elk City   73
Elk Prairie   78
Elk River   40, 78, 85, 86, 127
Elkberry Creek   91, 93
Esconobic, Michigan   60
Esterol, Ranger O.J.   100

Faucheaux, Bill   20-24, 76
FBI   32, 126, 143, 144
Featherstone, District Judge Albert   103, 107-110

Fern Creek 16
Fishhook Peak 10
Five Lakes Butte 22
Flat Creek 32, 41, 78
Flat Creek Cabin 34, 35, 43, 123, 142
Flatiron Knobs 10
Flodberg, Herb 46, 47
Foster, Arthur 113-117, 125
Francis, Mel 124, 125, 132, 134
Freezeout Mountain 76
Furey, U.S. Attorney Sherman F. Jr. 139

Gardner, Warren F. 113, 114, 117
Gerard, Jim 15
Getaway Point 9
Gibbonsville 73
Goat Ridge 23, 24, 75, 144
Goat Ridge Lookout 16, 19, 20, 65, 69, 76
Gold Hill 65
Gold Creek 78
Gourd, FBI Agent Stein 142, 143
Greer 12, 13

Hamilton, Montana 62
Hankins, Morris 139
Hansen, Fred 90-100, 103, 105-107, 111, 112
Hay, Ranger Ted 142-144
Headquarters 11, 13, 14, 31, 41, 70, 91, 94, 95, 97, 99, 101, 105, 110, 112
Headquarters Cafe 121
Higgins, Howard 26-28
Holloway, Sheriff V.L. "Slim" 100-102, 105, 106, 108
Holt, Louis 32-36, 42, 49, 58, 63, 68, 78, 82
Horner, Lee 43-51, 53-59, 63, 67, 78

Horseshoe Lake Lookout 74
Howard, John 82
Hughes, Perd 83-86, 91, 124-129, 151
Hughes, Ron 126-129
Humbird, John A. 70

Idaho Batholith 8
Idaho Fish & Game Department 43, 103, 126, 134
Indian Dip 8, 121
Iron Mountain, Michigan 66
Isabella Creek 16, 19, 20, 23-25, 75, 150

Jacobsen, Louie 120
James, Ranger Corland L. 3-10, 25
Johnson, Dick 47
Johnson Flying Service 47, 82
Jones, State Superintendent of Public Instruction Elton 130

Kelley Creek Road 4
Kelly Creek 74, 75, 137
Kent, J.B. 112
Kern, Chuck 123-125, 132
Kiiskila, Tom 134, 135, 138
Kimble, Prosecuting Attorney Frank 102, 103, 105-111
Kyle, David 34, 47, 48, 70, 74, 80

Lantz, Frank 82
Lantz's Bar 82
Leach, Lloyd 30
Lewis, Ranger Leroy 13, 16, 23-25, 29-32, 48-50, 55-66, 68-70, 72, 76, 77, 80, 82
Lewiston 13, 72, 82, 90, 92, 97, 144, 153
Little North Fork of the Clearwater River 27, 28, 87, 90, 91, 126

Lochsa Ranger Station   23
Lochsa River   23, 62
Lolo Motorway   74
Lookout Mountain   8
McCollister, Charles "Red"
   96-98, 105, 153
McCormick Steamship Co.   71
McCluskey, John   121
McIntyre, Paddy   2-5, 7, 8
McEachron, Justice of the Peace
   Charles W.   102, 103, 113, 115
McNichols, Ray   103-105, 110-112,
   114, 115
McQuade, District Judge Jack   103,
   104, 117, 118, 124
Marquette, Frank   30, 77, 121, 122
Martindale, George   15-17
Mattson kidnapping   32, 82
Mayer, FBI Agent Ed   70-73, 76,
   78-82, 142-144, 146
Meadow Creek Ranger Station   73
Melis, Clearwater National Forest
   Supervisor Percy   31, 34, 35
Meneely, Frank "Shorty"   49, 57,
   58, 60, 63, 66-70, 76, 78, 80, 120
Milk Creek   119, 120, 130, 137, 142,
   143, 148, 149, 151
Milk Creek Sub-Station   119, 120,
   147
Millard, Gerald   117
Miller, Holbert   85, 86
Mission Mountains   153
Monumental Buttes   77
Moreland, Bill   55, 57, 58, 60-84,
   86-147, 149, 153
Morgan County, Kentucky   60
Morrison, W.C.   60
Moscow Bar   77
Mountain Home   72, 79
Murphy Siding   69
Mush Camp   77

New Guinea News   81, 82
New Meadows   83
North Fork of the Clearwater
   River   9, 14-16, 36, 62, 83, 87, 90,
   92, 94, 100, 126, 147, 148, 151
Northern Pacific Railroad   16, 90
Nub Creek   59
Nub, The   22, 30, 75, 77

Oaks, Merrill   25-32, 65, 68
O'Keefe, Buford   90, 91
Orofino   11-13, 31, 35, 41, 70, 82, 100,
   102, 103, 125, 130, 131, 136, 145
Orofino Creek   13, 104, 151
Orogrande Creek   152

Peewee Cabin   25
PFI (Potlatch Forests Inc.)   90-92,
   95, 96, 99-101, 105-107, 110-112, 121
Pierce   13, 31, 35, 40, 75, 90, 120,
   121, 125, 147, 149
Pierce, Capt. E.D.   13
Pierce Hotel   123
Pierce Ranger Station   34, 46, 68,
   153
Pinchot Mountain   76
Pot Mountain   69
Potlatch Forests Inc. (PFI)   11, 13,
   86, 98, 103, 108, 109, 152
Potlatch Timber Co.   90
Potlatch Timber Protective
   Association (PTPA)   86-88, 122
Powell Ranger Station   62, 74

Red Ives Ranger District   25
Ridgerunner, The   26, 30, 32-54,
   56, 58-60, 63, 64, 66-68, 70, 83, 84,
   86, 91, 96, 98, 104, 111, 119-121, 128,
   132, 134, 144, 145, 148, 149, 151-153
Riley, Art   147, 148
Ripley, Bud   11-13, 15-23, 81, 153

Roark, Moton   34-59, 61, 63, 66, 68, 78, 79, 82, 83, 153
Rocky Run Mountain   8
Roundtop Ranger Station   3, 4, 7-11, 14, 25, 26, 30, 31, 42, 65, 75-80
Rutledge Creek   76
Rutledge Timber Co.   90

St. Joe-Clearwater Divide   8, 14, 19, 29, 31, 32, 75, 77, 90, 91, 122
St. Joe National Forest   1, 3, 26, 76
St. Joe River   4, 7-9
St. Joe Valley   8
St. Maries   4, 31, 144
Salmon Mountain   65
Salmon River   14, 65, 66
Sault Ste. Marie   71
Sawtooth Mountains   73
Selway River   64, 65, 73, 74
Shin Point   101
Shriver, Wayne   24
Shoup   73
Skull Creek   22-24, 36-38, 43, 49, 50, 56, 57, 62, 65, 67, 77, 78
Skull Creek Cabin   30, 31, 43, 44, 49, 55, 59, 77, 79, 133, 142, 145
Smith Point   76
Smith Point Lookout   24
Smylie, Attorney General Robert E.   130
Snow Peak   76
Southcombe, Dr. R.H.   115-117
Space, Ada   88
Space, Dwain   87, 88, 122, 130, 131
Space, Clearwater National Forest Supervisor Ralph   130-132, 134, 139, 140, 142, 146
Spokesman-Review, The   70
Square Top   65
Stars and Stripes   81

State Hospital North   130, 145, 146
Stillings, Clearwater National Forest Supervisor Fred   119, 120, 123, 130
Steele, U.S. Commissioner E.B.   80
Stevenson, Charles   113-115
Stevenson, Clarence   24, 31
Stratton, Ranger Herb   123-126, 132
Studebaker, Gilbert   114, 115
Studebaker's Mill   113
Superior, Montana   75

Teepee Creek   124
Tucker, Teddy   24
Turcotte, Louis   152, 153
Turner, Willmont "Arky"   15, 17-19, 21, 64, 75
Twin Creeks   77
Twin Creeks Cabin   8, 9

Urquhart, Ranger James   15
U.S. Army Corps of Engineers   151

Van Cleve, Dick   31

Wallace   14
Wallow Mountain   147
Weber, Baldy   32, 35, 43, 53
Weippe   13, 31, 32
Weippe Prairie   12
Welland, Whitey   101
Weyerhaeuser Co.   96
Weyerhaeuser, Frederick   90
Williams, John (Moreland's alias)   82
Williams, John (Forest Service crewman)   141, 142
Wobblies (Industrial Workers of the World)   112
Wolfe County, Kentucky   60